MY LIFE WITH MUSIC

Published under licence by Brown Dog Books and
The Self-Publishing Partnership, 7 Green Park Station, Bath BA1 1JB

www.selfpublishingpartnership.co.uk

ISBN printed book: 978-1-83952-147-8
ISBN e-book: 978-1-83952-148-5

Cover design by Lexi L'Esteve
Internal design by Andrew Easton

Printed and bound in the UK

This book is printed on FSC certified paper

MY LIFE WITH MUSIC

PAUL BRIMBLE

BROWN
D O G
B O O K S

STARTING OUT

Back in the year 1962 three of my school friends and myself bought guitars as we were going to be the next popstars. But as it turned out, I just didn't have the ability to learn and so I was volunteered to play the drums. I managed to locate a drum kit and if I still had them today they would be worth a small fortune. They were the type of drums you would see in the golden oldie movies of the 40s and 50s era – I actually paid £5 for them out of my paper round wages!

The drum kit was stored at the High Street Methodist hall at Midsomer Norton where I attended Sunday school and I played them when I could. I would like to thank Dick Milsom for letting me have a go on his drums at a youth club function at Fosse Way School. It left a lasting impression on me, so much so that I will always let children play on my drum kit – because you never know, if I wasn't allowed to have a go when I was a kid I probably wouldn't be playing now!

I first started playing, not on the drums, but on the washboard playing in a skiffle group back in 1961. I still have a washboard and the last time I played it was with a Bristol band called Bula Bula at a Rock'n'Roll weekend in Torquay 2005.

The first band I played the drums in was 'Rocking Olly and The Boys' and this was when I was still at school. I am not sure how many gigs we played at: it can't have been many, and most of these were at the Methodist hall youth club.

Paul Brimble

When I left school I played in a few bands, or as they were called back then beat groups, and was getting fed up of having this antiquated, old-fashioned drum kit and wanted a modern one. The drum kits back in the 60s had a small bass drum, either 18" or 20", not like mine which was about 30", and they had flashy colours – mine was boring!

I decided to buy a new drum kit, and advertised in the *News of the World* was a 'pay as you play' from Bell Music of London: a Gigster drum kit 18" bass drum, 14" snare drum and a pair of bongos all in blue sparkle – only £39 and so much a month. I did something I don't recommend and that was to forge my father's signature on the finance order and purchased my first brand new drum kit.

Me at eighteen

My Life with Music

I was now able to play with some decent bands, i.e. 'The Convicts and the Hermits'. We were due to play at the Savoy rooms, formerly Bob's Palais in Midsomer Norton when on the same day to our horror 'Herman's Hermits' were introduced on the pop page of the *Daily Mirror* – so that night we played as the band with no name.

Most of our gigs were at the Methodist hall, Orchard Vale youth club, the Savoy Rooms and St Johns church hall.

We moved to Orchard Vale youth club to practise, and as I only lived a quarter of a mile away I could carry my drums there and back.

The only photo I have of 'The Creatures'
(L to R) Dave Rogers (arm), Paul Brimble, Roger Coombes, Ray Rogers

One night I carried my drums from home to practise: it was pitch black and I had to climb a stile before walking across a field to get to the clubhouse. Then all of a sudden I rose up in the air and my drums and cymbals went in all directions: I had trodden on a cow and it had stood up, sending my kit all over the place. I'm not sure who got the biggest shock, me or the cow!

There were a few gigs that stood out from the rest: one was when we were called 'The Creatures'. We played at Marksbury, in the brand new village hall; I don't remember the gig for our playing but for the fact that I hammered in four six-inch nails through a piece of four by two timber into the brand new stage to stop my bass drum running forwards. (The caretaker was not impressed.)

We did, however, have a good gig at The Druid's Arms, Stanton Drew and this was 'Rocking Olly and The Boys', with Dave and Ray Rogers. We also turned up at the Naishes Cross pub Chilcompton (no longer there) one Sunday afternoon and put an electric cable through the window of the pub and set up the band in the car park.

One Sunday afternoon we were practising near to the five arches and the police from Westfield came down and stopped us, as we were playing too loud!

I remember watching many bands back in the 60s. I used to go to the Bath Pavilion on Monday nights when I could get a lift. It was a waste of time going on the bus as the last one from Bath to Midsomer Norton left at 10.00pm, giving hardly time to catch the main acts.

The bands that I did see were The Pretty Things, The Moody Blues (I was not impressed with them), The Who and The Kinks, whom I will always rate as one of the best live bands I have ever seen.

The Savoy Rooms in Midsomer Norton also had some good bands. I recall the singer Zoot Money and the Transatlantic Seven, also Dave and the Druids, Johnny, Mike & The Shades, Johny Mike and the Mexicans, Eddy Dark and The Salvoes etc etc.

Tony Higgins, Ray Rogers, Roger Jones, me

Until I was eighteen I had to rely on other people to drive me about. I thought I had sorted myself out a car when I was seventeen but the person I so-called bought it from didn't actually own it. The car was a split-windscreen Morris Minor and was a lovely vehicle, but Wimple, real name Tony Williams (a bit of a lad), had acquired it from a vicar soft-soaping him with whatever sort of story and then selling it to me. When I kept on for the logbook it became clear he did not have one and the vicar wanted his car back, so the first car that I owned I never actually owned at all.

I did eventually get my own vehicle but was not very lucky as far as passing my driving test was concerned. I actually had to take seven driving tests in total but only failed six!

I bought a split-windscreen Morris Minor van from Ray Rogers, one of my guitarists, and he had bought it from Roger Jones. It is shown in a photograph in this book with the Morris Minor car that I almost owned.

Me, Kate and Ray Rogers with two of the Morris Minors that I owned

I went on to own various vehicles which, if I owned today, would be worth a small fortune. My parents bought me a Vauxhall Victor, the model that had the sweep-around windscreen, bench seat and a column gear change. The car had so much rust under it that every time I drove it a bit more metal would fall off.

My parents went away one weekend. The clutch was slipping quite badly and I had seen a green Austin A35 van for sale at Wallmead Motors in Farmborough. I was able to do a straight swap for it; I kept the van for a long time, even getting my cousin's husband Ron Cray to fit a recon engine in it.

My brother Barry had a black Morris Minor split-screen car but had it damaged in an accident. He decided to get rid of it as it had a big dent in the driver's door and let me have it for a song; I kept it for a fair time. My next car was a Ford Anglia estate and I kept that for a while, but it turned out that the car had been so badly repaired before I had bought it that it was a death trap. The tyres kept wearing out on the front and I was told there was more lead in it than Dodge City. I ended up getting rid of it and I then bought another Vauxhall, this time a Viva and kept it for a couple of years until one day I saw a Goodwood Green Rover 2000 on the forecourt of Bences Garage Marksbury and bought it. This was luxury motoring to me and I kept this car for a long time, eventually giving it to my dad.

There were also the local bands: Bernard Emm and his Rythmairs, the Don Webb Band, The Saxtones, Ron Lamb and his Masqueraders. Also jazz bands: The Lazy River Stompers and Alan Moore and the Blue Jean Set, who were more of a skiffle group. (Alan went on to be an accomplished actor and was on *Coronation Street* for quite a while.)

The band that I tried to aspire to in 63–64 was 'The Cheetahs'. They looked the part, had the gear and a hearse with orange spots painted on it to take their kit to the gigs; not only that, Taff Matthews their drummer (the best in the area back then) also had a lovely Premier kit and I was jealous.

The Cheetahs: ?, Roger Peddle, Taff Mathews, Steve Webb

Paul Brimble

Every Friday there were bands playing in all the village halls locally and I am glad to have been part of it. I gave up playing when I was seventeen only for about a year when I started courting my first wife, but still had the drums set up in my bedroom and still practised when I could, which was mostly on Sunday afternoons after a lunchtime drinking session at the Kings Arms, Chilcompton Road, Midsomer Norton.

I did a Sunday nightspot playing the drums with a very talented pianist, Winston Church, who was playing piano for the Don Webb Band. I owe him a lot for teaching me all the rhythms for dance band music – sadly he is no longer with us.

Before Winston taught me how to play waltzes and quicksteps etc, I played a New Year's Eve gig to help out Ron Lamb and 'The Masqueraders', and I was reputed to be the worst drummer they had ever played with – but I was a rock drummer and had never played old-fashioned music before!

When I was nineteen our milkman Eddy Nott knocked on our door and asked if I was interested in auditioning for his dairy manager's new band that he was thinking of starting. He said that he had heard me playing the drums and put my name forward.

The outcome was that I passed the audition and joined the band. The personnel of the band were Gerald Sheppard on trumpet, Colin Smith alto sax and Derek Eels on guitar: the band ran under the name of the Gerry Sheppard Band.

The band was very popular and it was decided that a singer was required and I was given the task of approaching Carol Francis (formerly Carol Ball) who was a very good singer with a very good pedigree; she had been the singer for the Don Webb Band and also Bernard Emm – both well renowned dance bands. I was asked to approach her as she was a neighbour of mine and I knew her quite well. It was a daunting task but she agreed to join and we overtook the other main dance bands in popularity, as Carol was an exceptional vocalist and she even got to sing on television.

My Life with Music

The band changed their name to the Decimal.5 – pretty corny, I know, but everybody was caught up in decimalisation and we got away with it. The band grew in size over the next few years and took on a guitarist and a keyboard player and we supported some famous people. I can remember supporting Humphrey Lyttelton at the Shepton Mallet Showground, 'The Rubettes' at the Winter Gardens Weston-super-Mare, and Adge Cutler and The Wurzels at the Frome Car Auctions; we also played at the Imber Army Camp Warminster for Derek James and he had some famous Radio 1 disc jockeys there with us.

I built up my drum kit by using two Olympic single-headed tom-tom drums, white in colour, and as the rest of the kit was blue sparkle, it embarrassed me a bit. Then I had this bright idea; I bought a couple of rolls of silver kitchen roll and covered all the drums so that they would match and I carried on doing this for the rest of my time with that band.

We used to practise every Monday at The Lamb at Clandown and, even though I am not a reader, the band bought orchestrations for each instrument in the band for the up-to-date songs. I am talking the late-60s, early 70s – songs by Alan Price, Georgie Fame, Cliff Richard, Engelbert, Tom Jones, Tijuana Brass etc etc.

I remember when we had the bad floods in 1968 when the bridges at Keynsham and Pensford were washed away, we were practising at The Lamb and had great difficulty getting home, as everywhere was flooded.

Some songs were harder than others to learn. I was a quick learner: all the others in the band were readers, so it was not too long before the new songs were included in our playlists.

Carol was a quick learner. Sometimes she was stubborn in changing some songs to her way of liking, but she knew how to put a song over well.

'The Decimal.5' used to play at the Wells EMI Club and Carol got a mention in their national magazine for her singing. Gerald has to be one of the best trumpet players I have worked with, and Colin, although new to the saxophone, came on in leaps and bounds. When we first got together Colin was playing a white plastic saxophone and he eventually progressed to a real one! By all accounts the white plastic saxophones are worth an absolute fortune these days.

Derek was having private guitar lessons from Jack Toogood, a very renowned jazz guitarist, and he learned more chords than any other guitarist I know.

Bob Bridges and Charles Richardson, both guitarists, and Phillip Ford on keyboards joined the band, as did Sid Hodges, a tenor sax player. The band was one of the busiest outfits in the area: the only downside was that we worked a lot for the Derek James organisation and sometimes we only had a few hours' notice of gigs. Communication was hard in those days because not many of us had phones, but somehow we always managed.

I remember the power cuts of the early 70s and wondering whether we would be able to complete the whole evening's entertainment without losing power. I remember playing near Castle Cary and we were given an assurance that the electric wouldn't be cut off because there was a man on an iron lung in the village we were playing and he was on the same electric circuit as the village hall.

The furthest I travelled with the Decimal.5 was to Cricklade, near Swindon, but we travelled almost everywhere in Somerset, playing village halls, fêtes, dance halls, on the back of lorries, trailers, schools and even at the Winter Gardens Weston-super-Mare.

I was in my day job working as a pipe layer on a building site in Bridgwater, not getting home until 6.30pm most days, leaving at 6.00am for work in the morning – when we got the contract for the band to play six nights for the opening week at the Flamingo nightclub in Corsham, Wiltshire. Not only that, we also had to play on the Saturday night at the Assembly Rooms Bath for the SWEB annual dinner dance! You can imagine how tired I was that week.

We turned up the first night, and bearing in mind we had an eleven-piece band, the customers for the Flamingo only wanted the back line, guitars, keyboards, drums and vocals to play. We ended up playing The Stones, Beatles and Rock'n'Roll etc for all the six nights. The other players didn't need to even go onstage, let alone play – but were to get their money anyway. On the Sunday night I am afraid I lost my temper over it and said I would leave the band that following Christmas Eve. I don't think the band believed me, but I had made my mind up. I left The Decimal.5 at the end of 1972 and took three months off with a view to starting my own band. Three other members of the band left the following year. Bob Bridges, rhythm guitar, formed the band Scorpio, probably the best local band at the time. Charles Richardson formed a band named Sting, another very good band, and Phillip Ford joined the Bristol band Summer Rain.

During my three months break I met Andy Talkwolski who was an accomplished bedroom lead guitarist, having not as yet played in a band. He showed an interest in joining up with me if and when I formed a band.

I put an advert in the *Bath Evening Chronicle* and I got one reply. It was from Richard Doughty, a bass player: he asked if he could bring his mate Dave Stock, a rhythm guitarist, with him to the audition. I replied, the more the merrier!

I managed to get the upstairs room in the Commercial Hotel Midsomer Norton (now known as Mallards) to audition these musicians, and as I said earlier, Andy was only a bedroom player and I didn't even know Richard or Dave so didn't know what to expect. Once we were set up we decided to try out 'Johnny B. Goode', a well-known Chuck Berry song. You would have thought we had played together for years, we all gelled so well. We all agreed that we now had a band and decided to rehearse once a week. The landlord wouldn't charge for the room but asked if we would do a free gig for him when we were ready. We agreed to put on a gig for him and he invited lots of local people to the event. It was a Friday and during the night we were approached about playing the following night at Welton Rovers

Paul Brimble

Football Club which we accepted.

The following night we were asked if we would like to audition the following lunchtime at Westhill Gardens Social Club again. We accepted: we passed the audition with flying colours and were asked to leave our kit up as they wanted us to play that very night (four gigs on our first weekend on the road)!

When we had our first meeting Dave said he would do the singing until we could get a proper singer – that was 38 years ago and he is still singing for me! (This comment was made when I started this book: he went on until he retired in 2017 after 44 years.)

The gigs rolled in and we were averaging five gigs a fortnight but we still had to come up with a name. Andy was a fan of the band Yes and he came up with the name 'Spirelaine' which was a track off an LP of theirs. The name stuck and the band in various line-ups ran for 34 years.

The first line-up was:

The original Spirelaine circa 1973. Left to right: Dave Stock, Richard Doughty, Andy Talkowski, Paul Brimble

- Andy left after two years to go to university
– replaced by Kim Hyde on organ and keyboards
- Dave Burfoot joined as lead vocals
- Rich left and wasn't replaced

Dave Burfoot left, leaving Paul Dave and Kim until the band finished

For the last ten years of Spirelaine, Dave, Kim and I carried on as a three-piece band.

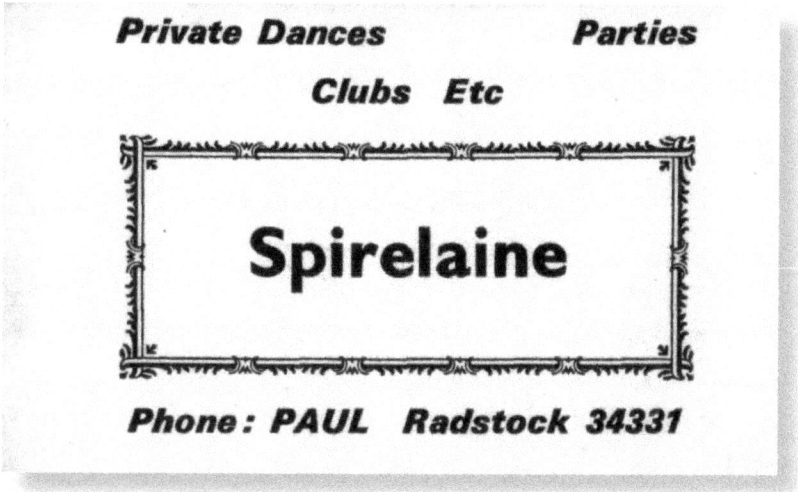

Business card for Spirelaine

There are many memorable gigs to recall: 'Spirelaine' supported 'The Barron Knights', 'Billy J. Kramer and the Dakotas', 'The Honeycombs', Frank Carson, Jethro, Ray McVay, Ken McIntosh, Andy Ross, Acker Bilk and Fred Wedlock – we even supported the Band of the Royal Marines.

BATH POST OFFICE SPORTS & SOCIAL CLUB
presents

DANCE & CABARET

at

THE PAVILION, BATH
Saturday, 22nd January 1994

7.30 p.m. - Midnight

Frank Carson in Cabaret

Dancing to "Spirelaine" Dance Band
and Mick McGinley Roadshow

LATE BAR • SPOT PRIZES • RAFFLE

ADMISSION BY TICKET ONLY
A D M I T   O N E

Tickets £11   No: 0095

Admission ticket for Frank Carson

Spirelaine started out as an up-to-date covers band, playing clubs and pubs.

By now, I had bought a brand new Beverley drum kit; it was grey oyster, from Assembly Music in Bath. I felt that I had now arrived!

All the band had pretty decent kit; the one thing we were lacking was a decent PA system.

We looked in all the papers and eventually located a Burns PA system, complete with three microphones and stands; the only trouble was that the system had a habit of surging in power and we were a bit nervous of it.

There was another band at the time doing the same circuit as us called 'Goldrush'. We got on very well with them and very often we would share the same gig. We did a fair few charity gigs with them and at the time they were buying a new PA system so we bought their old one, a Sound City PA system and we kept it for years.

'Goldrush'

oldrush: Paul Lapham, Ron Hagget, Mike Franklin and Bob Matthews, from the Radtcok area who took part in a special concert at Frome with three other local groups.

Gold Rush

The instruments that we had when Spirelaine did their first bookings:

• I had a Beverley grey oyster four-piece drum kit.

• Andy had a Japanese Jedson Les Paul copy guitar and a Yamaha amp; he soon bought a genuine Gibson Les Paul and a Fender Showman amplifier.

• Dave started with a Shaftesbury Rickenbacker 330 copy; he then bought a Guild SG and currently plays a genuine Watkins Rapier. He uses a Laney clip valve head or a Marshall Valvestate through a Marshall four by twelve cabinet.

• Richard had a Shaftesbury Jazz bass and eventually bought a genuine Fender precision bass which he played through a Marshall amp and four by twelve cabinet.

Paul Brimble

Dave left the band for about a year in 1977 and we needed to get a singer urgently. Richard and myself decided to visit Frome Town Football Club where I knew Dave Burfoot was serving behind the bar. Dave Burfoot also worked behind the bar at the Masons Arms in Frome where each Thursday night I played the drums for a mainstream jazz jam night. At the end of the evening he would sing the last few songs. He was a very good singer, a cross between Sinatra and Jack Jones: he blew me away and was to be on my shopping list for a new vocalist. The main stumbling block was his wife Maureen: I had been told that she didn't want him to join any band on a permanent basis. He had been the lead singer with the Bernard Emm Band for quite a few years and it had taken up a lot of his time and she didn't want him to commit to any bands.

Dave Burfoot

Dave Burfoot

My Life with Music

The night that Richard and myself went to Frome Town Football Club, Maureen must have been in a good mood because she said that it was up to Dave. Well, he joined Spirelaine that night and was with the band from 1977 to 1996.

In December 1978 Dave Burfoot had the flu and we had a booking in Wells. I was going to try and get by with Kim and myself doing the vocals when as I was driving past Dave Stock's house. I thought, "Why not knock on his door to see if he would help us out for the night?" His car was outside, so I chanced my arm. Dave was more than happy to help out, and, as it was December, said he would help us out as much as we needed over the Christmas period. After about three gigs I managed to get him to rejoin Spirelaine. We were now a band to reckon with – we were able to play big band and popular music. Dave Burfoot didn't enjoy the best of health and after almost twenty years with the band decided to leave, giving up singing altogether which was a shame as he was such a good singer.

Richard left the band in 1980, giving up music altogether. We had many good times together with Richard doing some memorable things. I bought a diesel van but it was automatic; not only that, to change from forwards to reverse the driver had to climb under the van and slide a bar beneath the engine and the gearbox. Somehow, one night Richard stalled it and couldn't get it to start so he slept in it. When he eventually got home about eight in the morning, Jane, his wife, thought he had just got up to make a cup of tea! Another time he was getting so much static onstage he wore Wellington boots one night and stood in a washing-up bowl (I am not sure why) to stop him getting shocks, I think.

Richard bought a Ford Cortina and the only way he could take his Marshall four by twelve cabinet to gigs was to put it in the boot – but he wasn't able to close it as the speaker cabinet was too big. One night on the way home from a gig in Frome I was driving towards Radstock when I saw a car through the hedge and it had a speaker cabinet in the boot. Sure enough, it was Richard, and at the bend in front was a Mini upside down in the middle of the road. Richard had braked hard to miss it, but it had been raining and he skidded off the road. I can still see in my mind the Cortina with the speaker sticking out of the boot. Dave Stock, who was following me, and I often have a joke about this even now, 40-odd years on.

Kim joined the band when Andy left to go to university. I knew him from Sounds International, the music shop in Frome where we bought a lot of our equipment: he was the Saturday boy and demonstrated the organs that were for sale.

'Spirelaine' did a Sunday night gig at the Masons Arms in Frome and I invited Kim to come along and maybe join in on a couple of songs as there was an organ in the pub. He came with his parents and ended up playing all night and agreed to join us. That was 1975 and he was with the band until their last gig – New Year's Eve 2004.

I formed 'Spirelaine' in 1973 and was working for a civil engineering company which at a later date turned out to our favour regarding transport, as I was allowed to use the works van to transport our equipment to the gigs. In the beginning, we all drove our own vehicles, but after about three years we had so much kit, Roy Rawles, who owned Sounds International, gave us his delivery van on the proviso that should he sell a large, electric organ I would deliver it for him as he now didn't have a van. (A good deal, I thought.) The van was a godsend and served us well. After a while it developed a strange fault – it would drive for so many miles and then it would cut out. After about a quarter of an hour it would start up and drive as if nothing was wrong. One day Dave Stock and myself were on our way to take part in a talent contest in what used to be the Top Rank Ballroom, Bristol. We broke down outside of what is now the Marriott Hotel in the centre of Bristol, causing a massive traffic jam. We were worried to death when a police motorcycle with its siren going pulled up behind us – but you could have knocked me stone-cold when the policeman took his helmet off and said, "Hi, Paul, what are you up to?" It was someone I had been to school with at Somervale Secondary in Midsomer Norton. He managed to get some more policemen there and they all pushed us round the corner, where we were able to get the van started.

We won the talent contest, beating a well-known Rock'n'Roll band called 'Chantilly Lace' – to be quite honest, they should have won but they lost on their attitude. The talent contest was for the Bailey Organisation: they had venues throughout England, with most having a resident house band, but in Bristol they had a resident DJ. Chantilly Lace were asked to back a singer from a well-known band called 'The Cougers': they were actually mates but said they couldn't possibly back somebody else as they needed to put all of their efforts into their own show on the night.

When we were asked, I said that if the singer knew four songs that we did but was not going to perform in the contest, we would back him. That is what happened and I think we won because we were helpful. 'Spirelaine' did quite a few talent contests and always got placed in the top three at all of them!

One of the many Spirelaine charity gigs

obbs, who is totally blind, and Alf Burden receiving a cheque for £130 on behalf of the Bath branch of ide Dogs for the Blind Association. The money was raised at a barbecue held at the Bear Inn, Holwell, d by the landlord and landlady, Mr and Mrs Neil Gregory. "Spirelaine" provided the musical entertainment free.

Me with my band Spirelaine presenting a cheque to Guide Dogs for the Blind
(L to R) Paul, Kim, Richard, Dave Stock

Paul Brimble

After doing the gig at The Bear at Holwell, where Spirelaine raised £130 towards a guide dog for the blind, I did another good deed for a mate of mine, another drummer Jim Scott – I gave him a lift home. On the way to Frome I was stopped by the police and was breathalysed. The result was positive and I lost my licence for a year (not only that, it was a leap year, 366 days!). Mary had to drive me about in my car during that year. Dave Stock and Richard shared the van driving but Mary drove the van a few times. A couple of instances come to mind, like the time she drove in the fog: we were on the Mendips and neither of us could see where we were going. Mary was driving slowly and vision was so bad that she had to stop. We got out to see where we were and if she had carried on would have driven into a lamp-post. Another time we were leaving Stratton Legion Club and Mary braked hard: the van almost went into a wall (I hadn't told her that the van pulls to the left when braking hard) and she was scared that all the kit would come forwards and crush us.

In the early days of Spirelaine, Neil, the landlord of The Bear at Holwell, put us into a talent contest for the brewery Courage (Western): it was under the name of 'Pub Entertainer of the Year'. My dad was alive back then: he was a part-time coach driver and he drove a full, 52-seater coachload of fans to the quarter-finals at the Viaduct Hotel, Limpley Stoke, near Bath. We got to the hotel. There were eleven bands entered and they all had their equipment in the ballroom; you had to see it to believe it, there were other acts as well as the bands. The bands that I can remember are Neon Rainbeaux, Sirrus, Goldrush, Sting and, of course, Spirelaine. All acts were trying to get into the top three as that would get them into the semi-finals at the Weston Hotel in Bath.

To make it easier to minimise the time needed to run the contest, it was agreed that some of the bands would share their kit with each other. At the time I had a brand new Tama drum kit and four bands opted to use them; the same bands shared the same backline amplification and PA system. Neon Rainbeaux had a full set-up of new Yamaha kit but wouldn't share it with anybody else and wouldn't consider using any of the other equipment on offer. I shall never forget Bob Frampton, their drummer, standing next to me on the stage as the winners were announced, saying to me that 'Spirelaine' stood no chance at that, his band were going to walk it! He was almost in tears when they didn't even get a placing.

Cirrus were a very tight, heavy rock band and had a very tasty drummer with the nickname of Bengo (I was very much in awe of him): sadly he is now deceased. The guitarists in the band were very good also but the band didn't last long together after the contest.

Goldrush were to me **the** band of the day. They took it seriously and their covers were near-perfect, so much so that when Peter Frampton recorded 'Show Me the Way' they even bought a pipe that fitted to the microphone – giving that special sound for the song.

I sat in with them at Southdown Club, Bath, one night and it was like playing with the jukebox – they were so true to the sound of the songs that they reproduced.

Sting were a very good band and had one of my mates from the Decimal.5, Charles Richardson, playing lead guitar for them.

Neon Rainbeaux modelled themselves on The Shadows and were a very tight band. The line-up back then was – Andy Weeks guitar keyboards and vocals, Des Edgell lead guitar, Alan Selway on bass and Bob Frampton on drums. I did feel sorry for them at the talent contest at The Viaduct because they finished their set with a Shadows version of 'Apache'; Goldrush started their set immediately after them with the Edgar Broughton version of 'Apache' and blew everybody in the room away.

Spirelaine could actually boast that they were pub entertainers and played a selection of songs for everybody; we even played a singalong and the judges were seen and heard to be singing along with us – and when Richard started making the animal noises in 'King of the Swingers' from the film *The Jungle Book* we were onto a winner. The judges ruled that it was the best heat that they had attended so far in the contest and decided to put four acts, not the three as agreed, forward to the semi-final:

1ˢᵗ Spirelaine   2ⁿᵈ Goldrush   3ʳᵈSting   4ᵗʰCirrus

We went on to the semi-finals and came third and were then put forward to play in the 'Player's No.6' talent show, where we got through to the semi-finals.

I decided that the band needed to dress the same and purchased some shirts. The first shirts had red and white vertical stripes, but were a bit drastic. I then got some more tasteful mauve ones and we wore these for a while. The next clothes I arranged were blue denim suits with very wide, flared bottoms: we still have a good laugh about these when we have the odd get-together. Kim joined the band, changing over from Andy, and had to take over his suit (Andy was tall and skinny and Kim not!). We then got proper beige suits and brown shirts and were always known as one of the smartest-dressed local bands.

Spirelaine in the recording studio

Dave Stock, Paul Brimble, Dave Burfoot, Kim Hyde

Spirelaine recorded two albums

The two albums were 'Memories' and 'Evergreen', they were recorded at the Music Workshop, Potterne, Devizes and were produced by Pete Lamb. 'Spirelaine' played in many venues over the years and I am searching into my memory to find them all.

Paul Brimble

Venues I have played with various bands

Arc Hapsford Club: One night when Spirelaine were playing at this club the dynamo went wrong on the Bedford van, and whilst we were playing the mechanics who were working on the night shift repaired it for us and it was ready to drive away at the end of the night!

Arnos Court Bristol: I played this venue with both the Decimal.5 and Spirelaine numerous times – with most of the bookings for either weddings or Masonic ladies' nights. I remember one night I was getting ready to drive there and I had been watching Mike Gregory playing in the World Darts Final: it was a brilliant match and I was almost late getting to the gig. Luckily for us, the speeches went on a bit.

Ashton Court Bristol: I played here with Spirelaine at the Mansion House, but only the once.

The Anchor, Warminster: The landlord of the King William was the son of the landlady of The Anchor and was looking for a band to play at the reopening of her pub after a fire had forced it to shut. He recommended 'The Sultans' and we went on to play this gig for a couple of years. I also took The Sneakers there, but with Tony Paul on bass guitar and later with Billy Colvin.

Assembly Rooms Warminster: I set the kit up in the daytime for one function here and went back to my day job selling windows. On the way back from my afternoon enquiry the gearstick in my car broke and by the time I had the car recovered I managed to borrow another car and got to the gig with only minutes to spare!

My Life with Music

Avalon Conservative Club: I played this venue a couple of times with Spirelaine.

Babington: The Sneakers appeared here twice, both times on the back of a lorry. The first time we did this gig we shared the evening with Martin Cox, a very good solo act. He ended up jamming with us: he was very, very good.

Bathampton: Spirelaine played in the back garden of a massive house. There were some very well-known guests – one was the actor Jack Watson. The host had a wheelbarrow filled up with ice and bottles of champagne.

Beckington Village Hall: I played this venue with the Decimal.5, Spirelaine and the Sammy Milsom Jazz Band.

Bristol 600 Club Hartcliffe, Bristol: This was with Spirelaine: we were scared to death because of the area but it turned out to be a good gig.

Bailey's Bristol: This is where Spirelaine beat Chantilly Lace in a talent contest. This club used to be called 'Top Rank' and it had a revolving stage; it was brilliant playing as we were moving. The van broke down on the way to the venue.

Bath Assembly Rooms.

Ticket for a Christmas dance

Paul Brimble

Purnell's Christmas Dance: My dad was one of the organisers for the Purnell's Christmas Dance, and had been for as long as I could ever remember. I tried endless times to get the Decimal.5 this booking but my dad said that as I was his son it would look bad if he put us forward. He didn't have to worry about Spirelaine as his committee put us forward themselves and we did the annual dance from then right up to its demise. Spirelaine played here quite a few times, always as a support band – they supported Ken McIntosh, twice. Also Joe Loss, Andy Ross and Victor Silvester Junior. (I didn't play this one as I was recovering from appendicitis.)

The Bear at Holwell: I played here with Spirelaine and I also played in the place of my nephew, another drummer, when he was in hospital; the band he played for was 'Howlin Dogs', they were a lot heavier than I was used to, with lots of Hendrix etc. I used to play The Bear every Tuesday with Brian Talbot from 'Just Uss'.

Bromley Heath School Downend, Bristol: I played there once with Spirelaine: it was for one of the local wine circles.

Bath T.A. Centre: We played this club in the early days of Spirelaine. I remember that during our break we would watch boats go up and down the river.

Bath Tramways Club: This was always a Sunday night gig, a bit of a nuisance at times, especially if you were out during the day and had to get back in time to set up and play. In saying that, it was always a good gig.

Bath Pump Room: I remember playing here for A.R.C. Quarries at a long service presentation evening: the acoustics were lousy. The Sneakers played here for a Masonic Valentine's dance and again the acoustics were bad. The last gig I did in the Pump Room was with The Sneakers; C.J. was ill and we used Bobby Hamilton, formerly singer/guitarist from Billy's previous band, 'Backbeat'. The gig went well, even though the acoustics were lousy. When I parked up after the gig there was a person standing up in my trailer wearing a miniskirt and fishnet stockings. I thought I had pulled until his wig fell off. It turned out he had been to a rocky horror show that evening, got drunk and also lost his mates, and so was hiding in my trailer.

Bodkin House, Petty France, Old Sodbury: This was the first-ever gig that Paul, Billy Colvin and Alan Braithwaite played together. They did so well that they formed a band called 'The Sultans' and went on to play many gigs together.

The Commercial Hotel (now Mallards): This is where Spirelaine were formed and practised each week, until they had enough material to undertake their first booking. We played our first-ever booking as a thankyou to the landlord as he wouldn't charge us for the rehearsal room. The date of Spirelaine's first-ever booking was Friday 18-5-1973.

Court Hotel, Emborough: Three times in a marquee, twice on a lorry and numerous times in the restaurant, again with different bands. This is where 'The Honky-Tonks' were formed. The Sneakers performed at the 2010 and 2011 court festivals. The Sneakers have also played in a marquee on the lawns a few times, once for the 50th anniversary of Massey Wilcox, the local transport company. There was also a 50th birthday party for Rob Wilcox. Two of the parties we played inside the hotel were for the local branch of the Labour Party and their guest of honour both times was our local MP. He shook us all by the hand and at the last one he apologised that there weren't too many people there. I said, "Well, that's the Labour Party for you." I must have been right, because they lost their seat at the next election. I also sat in with 'Hot Dog Jackson', when they played at the 'Techniglaze' 25th anniversary.

Paul Brimble

Coleford British Legion: Spirelaine played loads of gigs here. It is probably the best-sounding local hall to play in: the acoustics are brilliant. We did a New Year's Eve once and the snow was so deep that we ended up borrowing a four-wheel-drive vehicle to get us there. As it was, Kim couldn't get there but somehow we managed without keyboards, as you do. One night Spirelaine played at a football presentation and the organiser went home before paying us, he was none too pleased when Richard woke him up to get our money. The Sneakers have played here three times, plus a New Year's Eve booking for 2011. There are not many years that I haven't played at least once in Coleford Legion. It is the venue that I have played the most New Year's Eve bookings at.

The Bell Radstock: No longer a pub, it holds good memories for me – notwithstanding that I had my wedding reception there. I used to play drums with the resident blind organist, Pete Barry, on Thursday and Sunday nights for a long time, until he moved on. I was in The Bell the night Elvis Presley died and, with Sammy Milsom, played 'Love Me Tender' as a tribute to him.

Batcombe Village Hall: I was quite an easy-going bandleader, but one night when playing here Richard and Kim were having a dig at each other volume-wise. (Kim wasn't to use his foot pedals on the organ as it conflicted with Richard's bass playing.) They got so loud the rest of us couldn't be heard. I lost my rag and told them that I would leave the stage until they grew up! It worked and I didn't have that problem again.

Caxton Club Frome: Spirelaine did two gigs here every year for about ten years. I also played here once with The Sneakers. I've only played here once since my Spirelaine days. (The club has gone now.)

My Life with Music

Centurion Hotel, Midsomer Norton: Most of the bands I have played for have played here. I would like to make a special mention for Nigel Selway, who was the function room manager, for all of his help over the years towards all of us. I must add that it is a hard room to get into to set up. My daughter had her wedding reception at the Centurion Hotel and she ended up playing the drums in her wedding dress!

Article in paper

The Centurion Hotel was formerly the Fosseway Golf Club, and Spirelaine played here often.

Paul Brimble

Cameley Lodge: This used to be a nice place to play, but not now that it's got a noise limiter. In the past I have played with Spirelaine, Wishful Thinking, the Sammy Milsom Jazz Band and The Sneakers. I stopped taking bookings here, mainly because of the attitude of the proprietors, but was asked as a special favour to play at a '41 Club' function with The Honky-Tonks. I told them of my reluctance regarding the limiter, but was assured that there would be no problem. I was still concerned and arranged to set up at the same time as The Honky-Tonks. I asked Ian Hobbs, the lead singer, to sing. Well, the first word he sang tripped the electrics. I then bypassed the stage electrics by using a long cable fitted into a socket further round the room. Both bands had a brilliant night; the owners were annoyed as we didn't set off the sound limiter, even though we were loud. I don't think we will be playing there again!

Camerton Village Hall: This is another one of the halls with a noise limiter and now I always carry a very long electric cable to plug into sockets away from the stage so that our equipment doesn't get turned off when we reached a volume that put the traffic light system into the red.

Chilcompton Village Hall: Has a problem with sound. I have played here with quite a few bands. I even played here one night with a band put together for a retirement party. It turned out that the rest of the band, apart from me, were workmates of the person getting retired.

Chapmanslade Village Hall: The Decimal.5 and Spirelaine played this hall. Kim Hyde had his wedding reception here, the entertainment was by Deckchairs – a brilliant band – and for me it was nice to listen to another band.

Charlton Musgrove. It's in my diary but I honestly can't remember this gig at all.

My Life with Music

Cranmore Village Hall: Spirelaine played here twice: both times it was for David Shepherd, the famous artist. He asked me if we were the disco-tech at one of the dances. I said to him, "That would be like calling you a photographer!" I also asked him for his autograph. He said, "No problem." I then went on to ask, "Any chance of it beneath an elephant please?" He just laughed.

Clandown Football Club: Spirelaine were a regular band at this club, we had some brilliant nights here.

Codford Hall: Brilliant gig for Spirelaine but what a long way to go!

Croscombe Country Club: Spirelaine played here a couple of times and I played the drums with Brian Talbot a couple of times also.

Castle Cary: (in a marquee) Spirelaine played at a wedding in a marquee that seated a hundred people and also had a separate dance floor for a hundred people – it was massive!

The Centurion Bath: All I can remember about this gig is that it was a pig to get in.

Crossly Constitutional Castle Cary: I remember getting lost looking for this hall.

Evercreech Village Hall: I played here once with Spirelaine.

Conygre Hall Timsbury: I played this hall with the Decimal.5, Spirelaine, the Sammy Milsom Jazz Band and The Sneakers. Spirelaine did most of the Timsbury Wine Circle dances here. The very last night for Spirelaine was at the Conygre Hall.

Paul Brimble

Combe Down Services Club: I don't recommend playing in a sports hall: the acoustics were bad. I would have to think twice about playing there again.

Cumberwell Golf Club: Spirelaine, The Sultans and The Sneakers all played here, mostly for weddings and for Rotary ladies' nights.

Codford Social Club: The Sneakers played here once but a fight broke out; it was a very good night up until then. After the gig finished we were all outside on our hands and knees looking for a pair of glasses lost during the fighting – one of us found them. I don't think we will be playing there again.

Cases Social Club Dilton Marsh Westbury: I played here numerous times with the Decimal.5. Once was the night before I married my first wife.

Culverhay School Bath: We did a few dances for the Bath Wine Circle here. We did a Valentine's dance and at the end of the evening I asked if I could have one of the cardboard hearts hanging up as decorations. They were about five feet tall. I was told to take it on home and when my wife woke up in the morning and saw it hanging up at the end of the bed I was first favourite. But that only lasted until 10 o'clock – when I had a phone call for me to return it post-haste!

The Valentine's card I had to give back

My Life with Music

The Deaf Club Bath: (!) We didn't play for the deaf: the club was let out once a month to a dance club and Spirelaine were booked to play for the dancers.

The Dolphin Welton: This was where I played in my early days with 'Rocking Olly and The Boys' and 'The Creatures.' I remember one Sunday night the fair had been in town and the fairground workers had packed up and came to the Dolphin to finish their weekend off. I used to place the shove-halfpenny table in front of my bass drum to stop it moving forwards, and the fair boys each put a pint of rough cider on the table for me to drink. There must have been at least eight pints and I got very drunk! I've played the skittle alley there a few times but it is a bit small, more suited to a duo. In fact, I also played with Brian Talbot (a local legend) as a duo one night there.

With Brian Talbot at the Dolphin, Midsomer Norton.

With Brian Talbot at the Dolphin, Midsomer Norton

Paul Brimble

Downside School: I only played here once and the acoustics were terrible and the ticket prices were £50 each! (We were supporting Acker Bilk.)

Elm Tree Pub Westfield Radstock: I remember playing this pub with The Creatures, when an old man came up to us, shaking each one of us by the hand and saying, "Thanks, that is **the first time I have heard in years!"** I also played here a few times with both the Decimal.5 and Spirelaine in the pub and the skittle alley.

Farmborough Inn: I played here as a guest drummer with 'Just Uss'.

The Farrington Inn, Farrington Gurney: I suppose you could say this is where I formed a musical bond with Alan Braithwaite, Billy Colvin and C.J., eventually forming The Sultans who, in turn, changed into The Sneakers. Every Monday night there was a jam session in this pub and this is where I asked Billy and Alan to help me out for the Bodkin House gig. The Sultans and The Sneakers played here often and I jammed with numerous musicians over the years.

The Fir Tree, Writhlington, Radstock: The landlord of this pub liked The Sultans and booked us lots of times. I also played here a couple of times with the Pat Mallon Country Band. I also did a booking there with 'The Echoes', a Bristol band, for a birthday party one night.

Fosseway Country Club: I remember playing a wedding here and for some reason we were losing power to our electrical equipment – then at 11 o'clock the power surged. The heater for the swimming pool was switched off and the power was restored. We did The Lions, Masonic, the Rotary, Round Table ladies' nights etc. We actually worked there with Jethro before he was famous.

My Life with Music

Faulkland Village Hall: Spirelaine brought the roof down here; we set our kit up in the morning and when we got back in the evening the ceiling had fallen down exactly where we were due to play!

The Faulkland Inn: A bit small.

Farmborough Village Hall: Interesting hall. I first played here when I was about seventeen (I can't remember which band). I have played here at weddings, engagement parties, PTA dances and village functions. I have played here with the Decimal.5, Ron Lamb and the Masqueraders (this is the band that reckoned I was the worst drummer they had ever used), Spirelaine and The Sneakers. I also did a gig here with the Sammy Milsom Jazz Band, supporting the Pasadena Roof Orchestra!

The Old Farrington Gurney Village Hall: I played here with the Decimal.5 and Spirelaine.

Farrington Golf Club: I have played parties, weddings, Rotary, Round Table, Masonic and also fundraisers with numerous bands.

Frome Memorial Park: The Sneakers played here as a thankyou to Dorothy House, a charity hospice that helped my mum when she had terminal cancer – we headlined for a Lions Family Day.

Fenny Castle: We had some brilliant nights here; Dave, being the tallest in the band, had to stand on the floor because his head touched the low ceiling when he was on the stage.

Paul Brimble

Fortts Restaurant Bath: Spirelaine always played this gig for the Frome & District Motorcycle and Light Car Club at their annual presentation awards evenings.

Fosse Way School: This was where I sat on a drum kit for the very first time (the kit belonged to Dick Milsom, brother of Sammy). I am eternally grateful for this opportunity and always encourage others. One of our best nights here was a dance for the High Street Methodist Church and my old mate, Adrian Dando, the Midsomer Norton Town Crier, did the raffle. It was like having a comedian in cabaret: I have never laughed so much in my life!

Adrian Dando, the Midsomer Norton town crier, did the raffle

Adrian Dando, the town crier

My Life with Music

At the end of the night, thinking the gig was so good that we could 'walk on water', I said to the organiser Marjorie Gilson – who was my Sunday schoolteacher when I was a child – that I hadn't turned out too bad, had I? Well, I could not believe what she said next. She put her arm around me and said that everybody was allowed one failure and I was hers! I am sure she was joking.

Frome Police Station: The Decimal.5 and Spirelaine played here.

St Adhelm's Hospital Frome: This was Kim's first gig with Spirelaine after his initiation at the Masons Arms. When we set our kit up we saw some of the young patients in their beds and took pity on them so much so we gave back our fee – all but Kim's money as he had just bought a new organ and had payments to keep up.

Frome Conservative Club: we played in a skittle alley if I remember it right.

The Ship, Frome: Good old Des, he loved Spirelaine and booked us right up to when he left the pub.

South Parade Club Frome: At one time I had a double bass drum and a twelve-piece drum kit that was too big to fit on the stage so that I had to play on the floor in front of the stage.

Haydon Que Club, Haydon Radstock: Small but popular club. I have played here with The Sultans and The Sneakers

---

Hexagon Frome: Derek James ran this club; I didn't get on with him as he owed my previous band some money. Let's just say until he gave up the lease I did no more than I had to for him – but in recent years I have done quite a few gigs there and all have been good.

Paul Brimble

Frome British Legion: (no longer) Loads of good gigs here, Spirelaine played here for many years.

The George Frome: I played here twice with Spirelaine and also played here with some jazz bands that Shaun O'Conner had put together.

Mendip Motel Frome: I remember having a nosebleed playing here one night and was very lucky it stopped in time for me to play. We did a fair few gigs at the motel; it is no longer there after being completely burnt down.

Selwood School Frome: Spirelaine did some very good gigs here – it was a good hall to play in. I must admit it took a bit of getting used to having the bar by the side of us up on the stage.

Spirelaine at a Christmas function at Frome Town Football Club

Spirelaine waiting to go onstage

My Life with Music

We used to change in an old caravan behind the club in the early years. We supported The Barron Knights here on Friday 18-2-1977 and they were absolutely brilliant! I've also played here with The Decimal.5 and The Sneakers.

Oakfield School Frome: We used to get police messages through our PA system as the police station was right opposite.

Masonic Hall Frome: I have played this venue with not only Spirelaine, The Sneakers Wishful Thinking and The Decimal.5, but also other bands. It is the only hall where I felt the need to leave my drums in the middle of a song and put someone in their place because he was upsetting my missus and wouldn't take no for an answer.

Critchill School, Frome: Spirelaine played here for a caravan rally. I turned up towing my twin-axle trailer and parked it outside the school gates before enquiring where I should set up our kit. When told it had to go in the school hall I reversed the trailer straight back to the hall exit doors (about 150 yards), and this man came up to me and said that he had been presented with a certificate for reversing, but thought that my reversing was better than his!

Above the Pet Shop, Frome: This was for one of Kim's friends and we played there a couple of times.

Masons Arms Frome. This is where Kim did his induction for Spirelaine. I used to have to watch the landlady here as she would take my diary and put us in for as often as she could, but at her price **not ours!**

Frome Car Auctions: I supported Adge Cutler and The Wurzels with The Decimal.5 here.

Paul Brimble

Holm Lea Hotel, Frome: Whilst playing here we heard about the ferry sinking on its journey from Dover to France.

Enterprise Centre Frome: We worked with the great, late Leslie Crowther twice here.

Standerwick Market: Another venue where I have played with numerous bands.

Frome Memorial Theatre: Dave, Kim and myself backed the 'Old Tyme Musicals' here.

Frome Merlin Theatre: Spirelaine, Goldrush, Just Uss and 'Rockin Horse' did a self-financed show here – it must have been around 1976.

Fry Club: I have played the Fry Club with Spirelaine and The Sneakers. I also did a Country & Western showcase with the Pat Mallon Country Band.

Greyhound Hotel Midsomer Norton: The Decimal.5 used to rehearse here twice a week.

Glastonbury Town Hall: Spirelaine only ever played here once; it was for a Carnival Club's special year and we ended up with the 'Performing Rights Inspector' asking us silly questions like "Who wrote the songs we had played that night?" etc. We did give him the run-around a bit but got away with it.

Guyers House, Corsham: Spirelaine played a high society wedding here. The bride was a director on the television programme *999*, and the bridegroom was a television news presenter. I had a brand new Mondeo Estate car only days old and I felt like Jack the Lad – until I got to the venue where there were at least two Rolls-Royces, Jaguars and Mercedes all over the place so that took the wind out of my sails. One of the guests was Timmy Mallett and we backed him on his song 'Itsy Bitsy Teenie Weenie Yellow Polkadot Bikini'. I am sorry to say it, but he was rubbish; Kim, our keyboard player, had to keep changing the key where he wasn't able to keep in tune. However, there was a very good singer there by the name of Jackie Sheridan and we had been sent her music score a couple of weeks before the wedding. We supported her well and she didn't let us down, she was very good. At the end of the evening, after we had been paid, the bridegroom emptied his pockets of all the English money he had on him and gave it to us as a tip; he told us how much he had enjoyed the music.

Hawthorns Bristol: Played here only once but this was one of the in places of the 50s and 60s I believe that Pete Budd, now one of The Wurzels, and his band The Rebels were resident there for some time.

Spa Hotel Bristol: Again Spirelaine only played here once, another famous venue from the 60s.

Grand Hotel Bristol: Spirelaine supported Iris Williams at this venue for the Bristol Wine Festival. We were booked by Don Moss, best known for *Mr and Mrs* on HTV. Iris Williams was a fantastic singer: she hit one note and two champagne flute glasses snapped at the same time!

Holcombe Village Hall: Not very big, but a pretty good sound.

Paul Brimble

High Street Methodist Hall, Midsomer Norton: We got stranded out one night when playing here and if it hadn't been for Sally Clements, who kindly put three of us up for the night, I don't know what would have become of us. I actually got home about 7:30 the following evening and wasn't able to retrieve our van until the following Thursday. Thanks, Sal, much appreciated.

High Littleton British Legion: I have played this club with The Decimal.5, Spirelaine, and The Sneakers, and I guested one night with The Fretmen.

Hill Top School: Spirelaine played here a couple of times.

Keynsham River Suite: I only played here once and that was with Spirelaine.

The King William, Combe Down, Bath: I first played this pub with Pat Mallon and managed to get a gig for The Sultans; we played here until the landlord left.

Keynsham T.A. Centre: We played here in the first year that Spirelaine was going. They didn't seem to understand daytime from night-time. Just as well I was living in Keynsham at the time, because by the time we got away from this gig it was almost daylight!

Kilmersdon Village Hall: I did the opening night when the hall was built with the Sammy Milsom Jazz Band and have played with at least two other bands here since.

Kilmersdon Playing Field: I played with Spirelaine on the back of a lorry a few times and once we supported Fred Wedlock in the field. Fred was brilliant; there weren't too many people about, but Fred said that as far as he was concerned there could have been thousands there – he played his heart out. "Good old Fred, rest in peace." Once my son and daughter's band, 'The Young Uns', supported us and when it was their turn to play they were missing and had to be rounded up – they were on the bouncy castle!

The Jolliffe, Kilmersdon: We played upstairs in the courtroom a few times.

Leg of Mutton Hill Club, Glastonbury: I played here with The Decimal.5. As I recall the club was in the middle of a housing estate.

Limpley Stoke Hotel: I have played here with The Decimal.5, Spirelaine and The Sneakers, mostly for weddings and parties.

Locarno Bristol: Spirelaine played here half a dozen times – always in the Mayfair Suite upstairs, and what a job getting our kit in and out. We did a couple of charity gigs here; once we shared with our old mates Goldrush.

BRISTOL & DISTRICT SPINA BIFIDA & HYDROCEPHALUS ASSOCIATION

10th Birthday Celebrations

Thursday 10th June 1976   8 p.m. – 1 a.m.

MAYFAIR SUITE · NEW BRISTOL CENTRE

☆ ☆ ☆

Dancing to SPIRELANE and GOLD RUSH

☆ ☆ ☆

Complimentary ticket to admit one

Ticket for a charity

Paul Brimble

Longleat Stately Home: Spirelaine played this gig at Longleat House and there was a magician – he was so bad he was funny. I remember that when he put some large playing cards into his cabinet the spots fell off the cards onto the floor!

Mardons Social Club: Spirelaine only played Mardons once but The Sneakers thrived on good nights here. They were voted 'most popular act' and went on to play at three New Year's Eve bookings – at each of which Billy, our bass player who is Scottish, played the bagpipes at midnight.

Billy in full regalia!

Billy Colvin in Highland gear

My Life with Music

Marksbury Village Hall: This is where I hammered four six-inch nails into the stage. This was one of the first paid gigs I ever did and it was with The Creatures.

Midsomer Norton Scout Hall: I played here once, a bit of a pig to get into. **Midsomer Norton Ambulance Hall:** We played here one night and it flooded outside so bad that when driving through it after the gig the height of the water pulled the exhaust pipe off.

Melksham Labour: I played a few gigs here, nothing much to say.

Melksham Conservative: I remember the Conservative MP for Wiltshire telling us how much he enjoyed our band and could he come to our New Year's Eve booking, if it wasn't too far away. I told him that he was more than welcome, but as it was at Westbury **Labour** Club he might feel a bit uncomfortable.

Melksham Liberal Club: Pretty much the same as Melksham Labour.

Melksham Corn Exchange: Spirelaine played this twice both times for Masonic ladies' nights. Both gigs were good: lovely hall.

Moons Hill Quarry, Stoke St Michael: Unusual place for a band to play but Spirelaine played for Frome Rotary Club in a marquee at the quarry; we nearly lost the trailer in the mud as it had been raining hard. Good job I had four-wheel drive!

Midsomer Norton Cricket Club: I played here with Spirelaine often and also did the reopening night after refurbishment with The Sultans; did a few nights with The Sneakers who then went on to support The Wurzels at their open-air Bank Holiday Festival.

Paul Brimble

Moorlands Club, Glastonbury: Spirelaine played here often.

Midsomer Norton Community Centre: Spirelaine played a lot of gigs here; one in particular where we were playing a very loud song and we heard a loud bang. It turned out to be one of the bouncers breaking a troublemaker's nose. We stopped playing and Richard, our bass player, told the crowd we were not going to play again until they behaved themselves. I'm no coward but I hid behind my drums expecting a backlash, but they calmed down and the rest of the night was good.

Nettlebridge Inn: The landlord of this pub, Mike Perkins, was a sax player and often would hold a session with like-minded musicians and, as there was a drum kit in the pub, I would sit in with them.

Nunney Scouts Hall: All I can remember about this gig with Spirelaine is our old mate Henry Baulf helped to organise it.

Norton Hill School: I liked this venue as it had a sunken dance floor and a very large stage. Spirelaine played it a couple of times, once with a young band from the school.

Norton Down Church: I have played here a few times with the Sammy Milsom Jazz Band, always for charity.

Orchardleigh House: The Sneakers played many weddings at the house.

Perry Street Club, Chard: The Sneakers played here only the once; it was for a pre-1963 Rock'n'Roll night. I drove Billy and Dave this particular night and we got lost – but nowhere as lost as C.J.: we thought we would have to play without him.

My Life with Music

Priston Mill: I have only played here once and that was for a wedding. The Sneakers played in the watermill part of the complex.

Pilton Club: Spirelaine played here a few times and one gig in particular stays in my mind. This was the night after our van caught fire on the Longleat Estate. I have always been resourceful and managed to get our van repaired, but the outcome was that I managed to get another van for the Pilton gig – meaning we ended up with two. (Plenty of room for the kit, you would think.) But the following morning I got a phone call to ask if the red box left on the pavement belonged to us. It was only Dave Stock's four by twelve Marshall cabinet! It's about four feet square: you would have thought one of us would have seen it.

The Park Tavern Bath: I played here with Pat Mallon at a country jam session where I was the only drummer. This particular evening we supported many musicians, including Frank Yonco who lives in Bath but used to play lead guitar with Johnny Cash. The Sultans played here a few times.

Paulton School: Spirelaine played a couple of PTA dances at the school.

Winterfield Inn, Paulton: I did a Boxing Day gig here which was more of a jam session than anything else – using players from a few local bands. It was an all-dayer, but I really enjoyed it.

Lamb Hotel, Paulton: I played this pub a few times with The Decimal.5.

The Lamb Clandown: I did a few gigs here with The Decimal.5, as we used to practise there in the early days (it was there that I did my audition for Gerald Sheppard), but only one with Spirelaine.

Paul Brimble

The Red Lion, Paulton: I played upstairs in this pub with Pete Howe, a very good clarinet player and with a few jazz musicians.

Paulton Recreation Ground: Spirelaine played at a fireworks night on the back of a trailer: it was so cold Dave Stock had to wear gloves.

Pensford Village Hall: It's not very often that the person booking you is the local undertaker, but this was the case in Pensford.

Prattens Club Midsomer Norton: I have played here with The Decimal.5, Spirelaine, the Sammy Milsom Jazz Band, Bernard Emm, The Sultans and The Sneakers. When Shane was due to be born I made sure that Spirelaine had no bookings at the weekends either side of his due date, but didn't think he would be born on the right date – but as usual I got this wrong. Luckily I always set the gear up before the gig and on this occasion I set up on the Friday evening. Mary started getting labour pains the following morning. Shane was born at 2.30pm, and so I still was able to get to Prattens for the gig that evening. The rest of the band played 'Congratulations' as I walked in the room, and later we played 'Proud Mary' for my wife.

Paulton Rovers Football Club: I have played this club with many bands and have had many good nights. The club has two function rooms and I have played in both. We played here all the 34 years Spirelaine were running. It is a nice club to play in with very good acoustics. The band practised here for a year or two in the early days. I have also played here with Bernard Emm, the Sammy Milsom Jazz Band, The Sultans and The Sneakers.

Peasedown Football Hut: We remember very well a wedding we played here, as the electric was on a shilling meter and kept running out.

My Life with Music

Radstock Working Men's Club: The most memorable night here was a New Year's Eve gig when it rained in the morning and froze like a skating rink. I managed to get the trailer there and set up to play, even though the club wanted to cancel. I ignored my phone for the rest of the day!

The Rising Sun Godney: This pub used to get all the famous acts at the time (early 70s). Spirelaine got to play there once.

Red Post Peasedown St John: The Sneakers were very popular here, but the crowd were always boisterous and we didn't feel safe. All our bookings there now are in the lounge.

Rode Village Hall: Played here with The Decimal.5 and Spirelaine, mostly for parties.

Radstock Town Football Club: I know I played here but just can't remember it.

Rock Hall: How did we ever get in here!?

Radstock Victoria Hall: Dave Stock was taken very ill at this gig and was off for about three to four weeks. Luckily we didn't have too many gigs over that time, and what we did have we managed to cover.

The Redan Inn Chilcompton: I played here with The Decimal.5.

Regal Cinema Warminster: An unusual booking for Spirelaine. Kim had sold an organ to the owner of the cinema and had to show how good it sounded with the help of the band. The downside of this was there were only fifteen people there to enjoy it.

Paul Brimble

Rudloe Manor Box: Dave Stock belonged to a model aeroplane club and Spirelaine did all the dances for them and most were held there.

Somervale School Midsomer Norton: Spirelaine played this venue quite often, mostly for PTA functions. One night we did a gig with Goldrush and it had been raining hard. I had to drive the group van across the school grounds. Well, I got stuck and had to be pushed, causing massive ruts in the grass. The highlight for Somervale School for me was when, as an old boy of the school, I was asked to arrange entertainment for the school's 50th anniversary. I managed to get about eight acts having at least one member either still at the school or a past pupil. I obviously got Spirelaine and two of my children, both at Somervale at the time, were in a band named 'The young Uns'. Also got Chris Tabb, a very good blues guitarist (no longer with us as he died from cancer) and many more acts. I actually put an appeal out in the local *Somerset Guardian and Journal*, getting replies from all over the country. One in fact was a professional singer from up North somewhere – who at the end of the night said, "I enjoyed that but I didn't think they would have wanted me, as I actually got expelled from the school!"

St Margaret's Hall, Bradford on Avon: We supported Billy J. Kramer and the Honeycombs here. Billy J. Kramer was very good.

Trowbridge Civic Hall: I played here once and Spirelaine had 'Sounds Blue' to support us.

Tracy Park Golf Club: Played a wedding here with Spirelaine.

Station Hotel Hallatrow: I played a jazz jam night here.

My Life with Music

Street British Legion: The last time I played here was a party with The Sneakers.

Stothert & Pitt Canteen, Bath: I played this venue with The Decimal.5 and Spirelaine. One night Kim was unavailable and Dave Constable, a very capable keyboard player, helped out for the night. Decent-size audience.

The Savoy Rooms Midsomer Norton: I played here with The Creatures and The Hermits. This is one of the first venues I played in front of a decent-size audience.

St Alphege's Hall, Twerton Bath: This hall Spirelaine played a couple of times for Bath Wine Circle and it was funny to see these upright citizens coming out afterwards so drunk on home-made wine – I think you could have flown an aeroplane on it!

Saltford Village Hall: Again, a Spirelaine gig for another wine circle.

Shepton Mallet Centre: I played here with Spirelaine and thoroughly enjoyed it.

Street British Legion: I turned up with a brand new car with a different trailer one night, and when Dave Burfoot pulled up behind me, he almost went home thinking we had been double-booked! Another time, I had given my confirmations in for the bookings for the following year but with one omission, as we had already agreed with Street British Legion to play elsewhere on that night at a charity gig, so I had written consent to say that we would not be at their club this particular evening as we would be playing somewhere else. On the night my wife got a phone call wanting to know where we were. It turned out that the lady that did the bookings had put the confirmation letter in her handbag and hadn't used that particular bag since!

Paul Brimble

Shepton Mallet Conservative Club: Nightmare to get into, right on traffic lights. I also played with Brian Talbot there.

Shepton Mallet Showground: Spirelaine played this venue a few times and The Decimal.5 supported Humphrey Lyttelton here.

Sexey's School, Bruton: Spirelaine did the Christmas dance at this venue for about five years on the trot.

Southdown Labour Club: We played here often in the early days. This is where I played drums with Goldrush one evening.

Stratton British Legion: Many a good night in this club sadly no longer open. I played in four different bands at this club in one year alone. The only downside at this club was they had a sound limiter which cuts power to the stage if the volume gets too loud (we used to bypass the system by using an extra-long electric cable). The club were having trouble with the next-door neighbour over volume issues and Spirelaine were asked to play late one afternoon so that the council official could monitor the sound. He sent a message in to us to start playing – we had already done three songs by then, so he lifted the decibels instead of lowering them! The bands that I have played for in this venue are The Sneakers, Spirelaine, Close to the Wire and The Sultans.

The Sneakers at Stratton British Legion

The Sneakers in the early days

Street Unity Club: On the way to a gig at this club we took the wrong turning and ended up in the Glastonbury Carnival procession for about a hundred yards.

Showerings Club Shepton Mallet: (no longer) This club we used to call the 'paid practice' club as there was hardly ever anybody there, but we always got a decent price.

The Star Hotel Wells: This is the gig that I managed to get Dave Stock back playing in Spirelaine.

Trudoxhill Village Hall: I have played here with the Decimal.5, Spirelaine, The Sultans and The Sneakers. Most of the bookings were for birthdays and wedding anniversaries. We played for a birthday party here once and someone booked a strippergram: the person whose birthday it was got so upset so he told her to put her clothes back on!

Tunley Football Club: I played here a couple of times with Spirelaine – it is very small and, if I remember rightly, it was heated with mobile gas heaters.

Timsbury British Legion: Over a span of nearly 40 years I have played this club with many bands. It was also the club that The Sneakers played their final gig on New Year's Eve 2019.

Twerton Liberal Club: We used to play this gig about three times a year, but it was so awkward to get in and out we weren't sorry to lose this gig.

United Services Club, Frome: A pig to get in, but it was always a good gig.

The Viaduct Hotel: This is where Spirelaine won the quarter-finals of the Courage (Western) Pub Entertainer of the Year talent contest.

The Viking: I played there one night: it is really a restaurant and I don't remember what the gig was for.

Wanstrow Village Hall: Spirelaine played a Valentine's night here.

Westfield Primary School Radstock: I played here with the Sammy Milsom Jazz Band twice.

My Life with Music

Wells Golf Club: the Decimal.5, Spirelaine and The Sneakers have played here.

White Post Public House, Norton Down: I played here with the Sammy Milsom Jazz Band.

Woodlands Village Hall Longleat Estate: Spirelaine played many gigs here. We played here for a Christmas charity dance for Dorothy House; it was a very windy night and when we were performing, we had a power cut. Kim lit some candles and proceeded to play carols on the real piano and I backed him on the drums with the audience singing along with us. The electric was off for about half an hour. The funny thing is that we tried to re-enact it again the following year, but it didn't seem right with the exit sign lit up. One gig I remember well because our van caught fire on the way there; luckily it was near a puddle of water and I was able to put the fire out.

Welton Rovers Club: This was Spirelaine's second gig. I played here lots of times.

Westfield Club: This was to be our third-ever gig, but not before we had played at an audition that very morning. We played that club for many years and with Scorpio. Spirelaine were rated joint most popular band to play there at the time. I have played there a few times with The Sneakers, too, and one night I had the flu – but still played the whole night. Thank you to Shaun Whittock for helping me afterwards.

Wells Mendip Ballroom: (no longer) We got our first gig here by agreeing to play for the same cost as the disco that had been booked. We could only play sixteen songs but the band we were supporting, Blue Rhythm from Weston-super-Mare, were booed off and we had to play our set twice. We played this venue probably about half a dozen times after this.

Paul Brimble

The Wessex Hotel Street: Spirelaine played a gig here once a year for many years, it was always on Monday nights, as it was for the Somerset Butchers Association (they didn't open for work on Mondays). We fell out with them in the end because some prat decided to take out the speaker lead as he wanted to have a chat with some friends – he nearly blew up our PA system.

Weymouth British Legion: The Sneakers played here a few times; we even did a special night here to try and keep the club open.

Orchardleigh House with two of my grandsons

With two of my grandchildren at Orchardleigh House

My Life with Music

Weymouth Labour Club: A bit of a rough club but we had some very good nights there. The club has now been demolished.

Writhlington School: I have played this hall with the Decimal.5, also The Sneakers. One night I played the drums for Spirelaine **and** the Sammy Milsom Jazz Band for a charity dance to send Adrian Dando, our town crier, to Canada to take part in a competition.

Witham Friary Village Hall: Spirelaine played this hall a couple of times, one being Kim's first engagement party.

Wells EMI Club: Was always my favourite club. The Decimal.5 played here often and I knew the entertainments manager quite well, a man by the name of Len Rumney. When I decided to start Spirelaine Richard and I went out one Saturday looking for gigs and ended up at the EMI Club. Len told me that so long as we could play at least one waltz and a quickstep we were booked. So we went away and learned both. The rest is history, as we became one of the most popular bands to play there. I remember we were playing a song one night and someone won the jackpot in the one-armed bandit and the noise was louder than Spirelaine as it came over on Dave's guitar amplifier.

Wookey Hole Club: Unusual club, played it two or three times. Unusual as a third of the audience are actually situated behind the band.

Wells town hall: Spirelaine played it once, we were warned about the acoustics but had a good sound and a brilliant night.

Paul Brimble

Weston Ex-servicemen's Club: Another difficult club to get in and out of, but we did like playing there. Eventually we were out of their price bracket.

Weston-super-Mare Football Club: I got this booking from a family that had their caravan on a seasonal pitch next to mine in Dorset. I will never understand why people that live in seaside places go to another seaside for a holiday! Anyway, the gig was brilliant and we went down a storm.

Widcombe Social Club: Spirelaine only played here once, it was a New Year's Eve and we went down a storm. We actually got women out of the audience and let each play our instruments. What a row! But this went down really well. I think the reason we didn't get any more work there was because they only used agency entertainment.

Westbury Labour: A very popular club for Spirelaine: we played there for many years. One gig sticks out for the wrong reason: we were booked for a New Year's Eve and Mary, my wife, was pregnant and not feeling well at all. The band had set up in the morning ready for the evening and I had dropped the two Daves off at their homes. I was to take a rest myself, when Mary said she didn't think she would be well enough to go that night. She didn't want to take any chances, and, as she had miscarried earlier that year, I agreed with her. I decided to ring Dave Burfoot and offered to drive him to the gig. He was more than pleased as it meant he could have a drink. When I picked him up he was already the worse for wear as he had been drinking all afternoon. We tried to sober him up and he only drank black coffee all night. We managed to get through the night but I was very cross!

Westbury Railway Club: I played this club for a couple of years, never really made our mark here.

My Life with Music

Westbury Blue Circle: Brilliant club until the steward decided to start and finish early, which meant Dave Stock had to pick Kim up just before 7 of a Saturday evening, to be ready for an 8 o'clock start. We had already been out in the morning to set up as well!

Centenary Club Weymouth: This was a good club. The Sneakers had some brilliant nights there; but the club ended up with a very corrupt committee and it all ended in tears.

Writhlington Village Hall: Only once here, but it was a good gig.

Yeovil Labour: Roger McCourtney – a brilliant lead guitarist – asked me if Spirelaine would play with him for three gigs at this club. We had never played here before, so I arranged for Dave Stock and me to check the club out. Shaun, the entertainments manager, really made us feel at home and we looked forward to playing there. On the first of the bookings Dave and myself went to Yeovil in the afternoon to set up and we were ready when Roger got there. Kim arrived later and his Rotary cabinet started to cause problems so that Kim became agitated. He stated that Yeovil was too far to go for a gig and basically spoilt the night for the rest of us. He was far too loud and drowned Roger out on his guitar solos, so much so Roger decided he didn't want to play the other two bookings. I was very annoyed with Kim's attitude and decided not to put Spirelaine back in Yeovil Labour Club again but, with Shaun's permission, would put The Sultans in their place. The Sultans went down very well and got more bookings; it was there that Alan Braithwaite put C.J. in to cover for him. We then changed eventually to The Sneakers with C.J. as our regular singer/guitarist. I thought that putting three bands in that club was good – but I was then asked if I could put a band together to help them out as another band had let them down at the last minute. I managed to get Billy Colvin and Frank Aust to form a band with me for the one night and called ourselves 'Three of a Kind' – we went down a storm! The Sneakers also played each year for the Burns Night celebrations and Billy piped in the haggis and also did the toast.

BIRTHDAYS

My 40th birthday party was held at The Jolliffe Arms, Kilmersdon

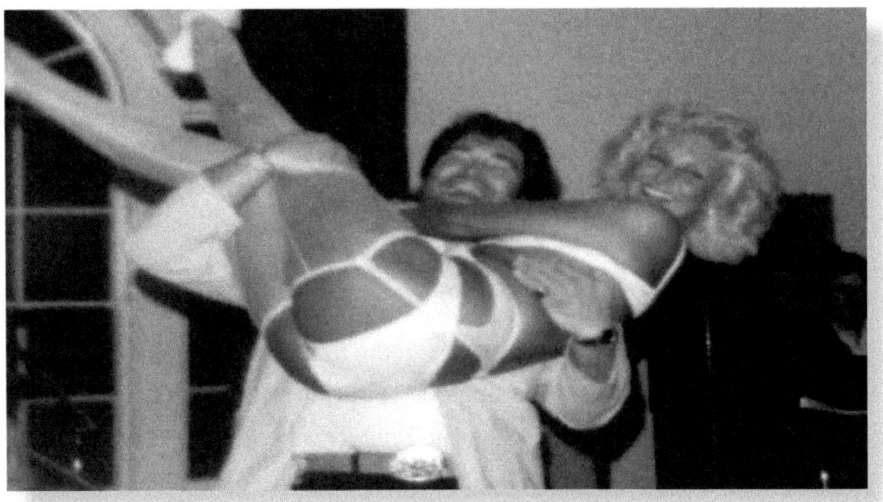

Me with strippergram

My 40th birthday party was held at The Jolliffe Arms, Kilmersdon, and Graham Long was employed to play organ, guitar and to sing. Spirelaine played the rest of the evening. There was a surprise entertainer – a strippergram. My daughter, who was only three at the time, jumped up into my arms and said, 'Send that strippergram lady away, only my mummy kisses my daddy!'

God only knows what could have happened. Mary said she was a dog anyway!

My Life with Music

ENOUGH CANDLES TO BURN THE PUB DOWN!

With my 40th birthday cake

My 50th party: I had eight bands play at this party, held at Welton Rovers Football Club. Some of the musicians were from the Monday night jam sessions at The Farrington Inn.

The evening started with Jeremy Hole and Martin Shepherd. With the other drummer, they played mostly Rock'n'Roll.

The next band was 'Close To The Wire', which featured Joe Bennett, the technical editor for *Total Guitar* magazine on lead guitar (very tasty), Kevin Rowe on bass, Paul Kirtley electro-acoustic/vocals, and me on drums.

Paul Brimble

Paul Kirtley, me, Kevin Rowe, Joe Bennett

The 'Young Uns' reformed for the night. This was a very proud moment for me as both my son Shane, guitar and vocals, and daughter Georgii, on the drums, joined together with Lee Williams on bass and vocals, with Ben Bridges on lead guitar.

Ben Bridges, Lee Williams, Shane Brimble, Georgii Brimble at my 50th

Andy Talkowski, Dave Stock, me, Kim Hyde at my 50th

John Williams, me, Dan Seward, Simon Carder at my 50th

Paul Brimble

Lee Williams with Shane and friends at my 50th.

Andy came down from Sheffield and Richard, both former members of Spirelaine from the early days. Dave Burfoot, also a former member of Spirelaine, and Shaun O'Conner, a well-known bass player from Frome. I employed a drummer from Wiltshire to play when I needed a break, as I was to play with most of the bands that night. I played with Kim Hyde and Dave Stock (which was then and up to their demise the line-up for Spirelaine); we were then joined by other former members, Andy Talwkoski, Richard Doughty and Dave Burfoot, to make up the biggest line-up we had.

Jamming musicians at my 50th

My Life with Music

The other three bands were made up from the jammers from The Farrington Inn, and at the end of the evening we had as many people onstage as possible playing! Including me and the other drummer, there must have been at least six lead guitarists, and three bass players; also Simon Carder, the best harmonica player in the West, plus at least six singers. The song we were playing was 'Johnny B. Goode'. (I wish that there was a video camera handy.)

Jamming musicians at my 50th

My wife Mary's 40th surprise birthday party: I booked Silver Lining to play with Spirelaine and was very impressed with their drummer, for the fact not only that he was into his seventies, but also that played very well and fitted in very well with the other two. The guitarist was his son Steve Shearn. This was the first time my son, Shane, ever had a go on a drum kit and what a row.

Paul Brimble

The first time Shane sat on a drum kit

Mary's 50th surprise birthday party: This party was held at Midsomer Norton Cricket Club and Spirelaine again supplied the entertainment. Mary was under the impression that I was doing nothing for her – so much so she moaned over the fence to our next-door neighbour. She was stating that I wasn't doing anything, at least like taking her out for a meal, or to a show or something! Well, Peter, our neighbour (a retired vicar), had to explain later in the speech that I had asked him to fib to her that he wasn't a 'bad chap after all' and that he hoped he will still go to Heaven, even if he had to tell a little white lie!

Andy Talkowski had his 40th birthday at Southwick Village Hall and Spirelaine did a reunion with Andy on lead guitar. He also had a reunion with his other band 'Dr Mo'. My son and daughter did their first-ever show in public: they played 'Apache' with Shane on guitar and Georgii on drums.

My Life with Music

Dave Stock celebrated his 60th surprise birthday party at the New Farrington Gurney Village Hall with Spirelaine and Brian Talbot.

Ray Rabbit's 50th birthday Orchard Vale Hall – this night Spirelaine did get an eyeful of the strippergram as she turned her back on the audience! Pity, it was the same dog! That did my 40th. The funniest thing that happened that night was that Ray's mother-in-law chased him out of the building for enjoying the stripper.

Jenny, Billy's missus, had her 50th at Welton Rovers Football Club and The Sneakers played for her.

Billy had his 50th at Mardons Social Club and The Sneakers played for him, as did a young band which also included one of his pupils.

Chris, the lead guitarist/vocalist for The Sneakers, had his 50th surprise birthday party in the Centenary Club, Weymouth, and ended up playing at his own party with The Sneakers.

Weddings: Spirelaine did a wedding at a golf course near Frome: it was quite a well-heeled affair. An estate agent from Frome – and also a nightmare as far as taking the kit in was concerned as it was upstairs!

Orchardleigh House: The Sneakers played the first-ever wedding that was held there and went on to do more: one was for the landlord of The Red Post at Peasedown St John, and they also played for Mary's sister Andrea when she got married there.

The poshest place Spirelaine did a wedding was Bowood House, but they did other gigs at Marston House and Longleat and also at the Plymouth Pavilions.

THE NEXT GENERATION

My eldest son Adrian (Charlie), a very good lead guitarist, with his first guitar

Adrian (Charlie), my eldest son with his first guitar

Charlie playing acoustic guitar

Charlie playing an acoustic guitar

My Life with Music

His favourite guitar, a genuine American Fender Telecaster

Charlie with his Telecaster (his pride and joy)

Having a Hank Marvin moment

Charlie having a Hank Marvin moment

Paul Brimble

Charlie joining in with others

At my 60th birthday party
My youngest son Shane, starting young

Shane was the first of my children to show promise regarding music. He started piano lessons at the age of eleven and achieved quite a high standard. The local St John Ambulance Division invited up and coming talent to enter their talent contest. Shane entered and did quite well – so much so he entered again the following year, as did Georgii. One of the judges was Elise Rayner, a presenter from HTV.

My Life with Music

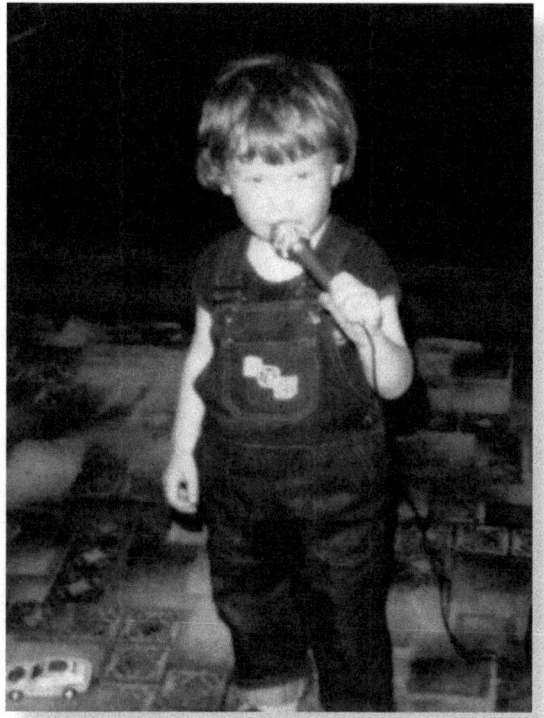

Shane started young

This was Shane's thirteenth birthday and he came first. Not long after the competition, Shane became disinterested in playing the keyboards anymore and stopped having lessons. Just before Christmas this particular year I went to a car boot sale in Frome and bought an electric guitar. It was damaged and I managed to get it for a tenner, knowing that I could repair it myself! I gave it to Shane at Christmas, with all of his other presents, and on New Year's Eve I took him to my brother-in-law, Mike Chant, who used to be lead guitarist for the band 'Rockin Horse'. He tidied the guitar up and put a new set of strings on it, and he also taught Shane three chords.

Paul Brimble

Shane competing in a talent competition with one of the judges

Shane when he won a talent contest

Elise Rainer, one of the judges

My Life with Music

Shane performing with his guitar teacher Billy Colvin

Billy Colvin and Shane playing at Georgii's wedding

Shane playing a song for his sister at her wedding

Shane playing at his sister's wedding

Paul Brimble

I moved the following March to a house with a garage: this was 1994. One day I heard a guitar being played in the garage and called my wife to have a listen. It was Shane: he had plugged into one of my amplifiers and was playing 'Apache' by The Shadows, and I was very impressed that he had taught himself to play it. I asked Shane if he would like some guitar lessons, he said that he would, but didn't think that I would buy him some after he had stopped his piano lessons so abruptly.

I told him that I would try to find a guitar teacher, and started asking around and the same name kept coming up. A person by the name of Billy Colvin who lived at Haydon, near Radstock. Mary, my wife, took him for his first lesson and when she came back she said that Billy had hair even longer than mine!

Shane had lessons for quite a while, until I found out he was jamming with Billy and it was costing me a fortune.

Charlie started showing an interest and he, too, started having lessons with Billy and got to a very high standard. He also bought some nice guitars.

Shane and Georgii, with our old neighbours Lee Williams and Caleb Taylor, started their own band. They called themselves 'The Young Uns' and I converted my garage to accommodate them. The following Boxing Day I was asked to share the drumming with Choochy Hurle as his band, Hair of the Dog, were playing at The White Hart, Midsomer Norton all the afternoon and into the evening (too long for one drummer) so I agreed.

I arranged to walk down to The White Hart with Shane and Georgii who were to meet up with Lee Williams off the bus. When I got to the pub I bumped into one of my old Decimal.5 mates, Bob Bridges, who had his son Ben with him. Bob said that Ben had been having guitar lessons at school and that he had bought him an electric guitar for Christmas. I asked Bob if Ben wanted to go back to my house with the others as they were going to practise and he agreed to go with them.

About teatime I was playing on the drums and the kids came in: they said that they had learned four songs and could they play them in the pub? I managed to get them permission. Whilst they played, I was sitting on a stool at the rear of the room when Tony Docherty, a local character, came up to me and said, "What do you think of these?" I said, "I feel ten feet tall as two of them are mine!"

Subsequently they played the Midsomer Norton Mardi Gras and numerous other gigs until Shane and Lee broke away and formed Prolo.

Shane has played in many bands and at this time of writing is playing drums for 'Ulysses' and has played The Cavern, Liverpool a few times. Charlie, although a very good guitarist, doesn't play in any bands but he did get onstage at my 60th birthday party with Shane, Billy and Jaydon, his eldest son, seven at the time.

Me with Tony Docherty

Tony Docherty, a local character

Paul Brimble

"What do you think of these?" – "I feel ten feet tall, as two of them are mine!"

My daughter Louise (Georgii) aged ten.

Georgii

Bride beats the drums at a rocking reception

THE BRIDE played the drums with her father's band after the wedding of print manager Lee Marcus Tustin and nursery nurse Louise Marie Brimble, from Westfield.

The wedding ceremony took place at St John's Church, Midsomer Norton, on April 7.

The bride wore an ivory corset dress with beaded detail at the front and criss-cross straps at the back.

Her flowers were cream and lilac lilies, arranged by her aunt.

She was attended by the maid of honour, her best friend Linsay Gilleland, and bridesmaids Zoe and Katie Hill, the groom's cousins. The couple's daughter, Georgia Tustin, was the third bridesmaid.

Pageboys were Jaydon and Corey Brimble, the bride's nephews. Best man was Scott Tustin, the groom's brother.

A reception was held at the Centurian Hotel, Midsomer Norton, where guests were entertained by the bride's father's band and the bride herself on the drums.

The bride's mother made the newly-weds a beautiful wedding cake.

The couple, who met as neighbours in a classic "boy next door" romance, left after the celebrations for their honeymoon destination, Newquay in Cornwall.

The parents of the groom, Ivor and Ruth Tustin, from Midsomer Norton, and parents of the bride, Paul and Mary Brimble, also from Midsomer Norton, would like to congratulate the happy couple.

BOY NEXT DOOR: Louise Brimble and Lee Tustin were married at St John's Church, Midsomer Norton, on April 7 PICTURE: Lorraine Nevill

Article in local paper

My Life with Music

There was a Sunday jam session advertised at The Somerset Arms, Maiden Bradley, and I called in to see if The Young Uns would be allowed to play there. Willy, the landlord, welcomed them with open arms and they became a regular feature. They even got to play at an outside festival in the grounds of the pub. I got to know and play with some very good musicians there and made very good friends with Taffy, who was the resident drummer. He in fact ran the jam sessions and had a drum kit I would have given my right hand for: in fact, I tried to buy it on numerous occasions. Both of us shared the drumming and the jam sessions went on for many months until, like any other good thing, it had to come to an end. The jam sessions then moved to the Masons Arms in Warminster but it wasn't the same and eventually fizzled out. Don't get me wrong, I've had some really good sessions there, but the whole concept wasn't the same.

The Young Uns. Left to right: Ben Bridges, Lee Williams, Georgii Brimble, Shane Brimble

The Young Uns, minus Caleb, went on to do eighteen months of busy gigging as the youngest rock band in the country. They appeared on television, were auditioned by Sherrie Eugene-Hart from HTV, and performed on a TV programme called *Spotlight*, where one of the other acts was Boyzone.

The Young Uns with Sherrie Eugene-Hart from HTV Television

Radio Bristol. Shane, Lee and Georgii swapped instruments during their sets and Shane became a very accomplished drummer and in my opinion is better than me. Georgii was very good on the bass, too.

The Young Uns' first-ever jam at the Somerset Arms

My Life with Music

BANDS I'VE PLAYED IN

Talking about jam sessions, The Farrington Inn at Farrington Gurney started jam sessions on Monday nights. I decided to go and, as it turned out, one of my old mates – a brilliant blues guitarist, Alan Braithwaite – was running the sessions. This jam session ran for a few years and the landlord of the pub was the resident drummer: he was quite tidy on the kit. His name was Nick Nicholsan and his claim to fame was that his band, Chet and the Zephyrs, actually supported The Beatles in the Bath Pavilion.

Nick and myself did most of the drumming, but often other drummers turned up and helped out. Like most jam sessions there were always regular players, so there were always ready-made bands to entertain.

Alan Braithwaite at the time was playing lead guitar for The Beatles tribute band, Backbeat, and their bass player, Billy Colvin, was the guitar teacher that taught both my sons to play guitar. Spirelaine had taken a booking for a wedding at the Bodkin House, Petty France, and it was through an agency. I had a call from Kim to say that he would not be able to do the gig: I didn't want to lose the booking as it was well paid. The people getting married had never seen or heard the band so I decided to approach Alan and Billy and get them to play their Backbeat set, with me playing the drums using my Ludwig Vistalite kit with the name Spirelaine on the front, and they agreed to do it.

Not only did we get away with it, but we also picked up some more work from it and decided to form a band to play any gigs that might come our way. There is a humorous tale to this story as I took another booking at the Bodkin House and neither Alan nor Billy could do it so I took the original Spirelaine to play. The manager of the hotel said we were very good, just like the last time! Just goes to show, doesn't it?

Around the year 2000 I started to get a little fed up with the rut Spirelaine had got themselves into and started going to a jam session for musicians every Monday night in The Farrington Inn. I started to come alive, playing all genres of music. So much so I started helping other bands out when they needed a drummer. At one time I was playing in nine different bands: rock, jazz, country, heavy rock, Rock'n'Roll, dance band, pop covers and blues.

Some of the bands that I have played for:

Rocking Olly and The Boys: the first band I was in with brothers, Ray and Dave Rogers.

The Creatures: this is the band that rehearsed at Orchard Vale youth club and we had numerous line-ups.

The Hermits: born out of the creatures.

The Decimal.5: I was in this band for five years and it was the main turning point in my drumming career.

Spirelaine: this band was my baby. I ran it for what must be near on a record. Mind you, it was like Trigger's brush in *Only Fools and Horses* with the few different line-ups we had. The band went on for 34 years and, apart from four weeks at the end of 1978 when I had an emergency operation for gangrene appendix, I have played every booking. Even six days after I had a mild heart attack, Christmas Day 1999, I went on to play at a Millennium booking.

Goldrush: in 1973 this was the best band in our area, without doubt. I played with them one night and they were so perfect it was like playing to the jukebox.

My Life with Music

Six days after my heart attack

Sammy Milsom Jazz Band: Sammy was a legend in his own time, I loved him to bits. I could tell so many stories about him, but I won't – apart from saying all the gigs I did with him were memorable for various reasons (sadly now deceased). When someone like Acker Bilk says, "If Sam was a bit younger I would have him in my band" (they were the same age), you knew you were playing with an icon!

Rocky Tops: Barry Bevan, this was his band. I can't say that I really enjoyed playing with him as he had a bad habit of playing over the bars, causing many timing problems for me. In fairness to Barry he had a nice voice and was very popular with his following.

Bernard Emm: I got to know Bernard well in his later years and got to play with his band a few times and once, with Bernard on piano, Sammy Milsom on trumpet and myself on drums, played at a wedding reception at The Talbot Inn, Mells, we played a blinder. I asked Sammy one day what Bernard Emm thought of my drumming. He said that young Brimble never gets in the way when the band is playing. He said that is as good as a compliment coming from Bernard, as he doesn't very often give any.

The Masqueraders: this is the band that thought I was the worst drummer they had ever worked with. Enough said!

The Sultans: this band featured one of the best lead guitarists I have had the privilege to have worked with – Alan Braithwaite. I first met Alan when he first started to play guitar – in fact, I sold him his first electric guitar. Not only this, it turns out that Dave Stock, my rhythm guitarist, taught him his first chords.

The Sneakers: one of the best bands I have ever played for, but I am a bit biased.

Love in a Hanky: this was a band put together at the jam session at the Masons Arms, Warminster.

Close to the Wire: this was a band of quality players. Paul Kirtley on vocals and rhythm guitar; he was also a talented songwriter. Kevin Rowe on bass guitar. Joe Bennett on lead guitar, who was also technical editor for *Total Guitar* magazine, a 'needs must' quality magazine for all guitarists.

Pat Mallon Big Country Band: what can I say about Pat Mallon? I first met Pat at the jam sessions at The Farrington Inn and he asked if I would play the drums for his country band at a Country and Western night at Cinderford Town Football Club. He said that he liked my aggressive style of playing and that I would suit his band fine. When we got to the gig it turned out that the band were put together for that night only and, even though most of the band knew each other, they hadn't seen one another for years. Pat expected me to play with a drum machine: I managed one song with it and when he wasn't looking, I pulled the plug out. That night I met Colin Lewis a very capable lead guitarist who went on to form Beach Boys Incorporated and The Mersey Makers, both very talented bands. Pat explained that he suffered from 'PMT' – Pat Mallon timing. The night went well and we got rebooked; this time the line-up included Dave Stock, Tony Paul and Roger McCourtney – all musicians I have played with in various bands over the years. (Pat sadly no longer with us.)

Just Uss: I used to play the drums with Brian Talbot from Just Uss every Tuesday at The Bear at Holwell and have done numerous gigs with Just Uss over the years.

The Worried Men: one Friday afternoon I was at work and was told that 'a person by the name of Jamie' was holding on the phone for me. I was on the phone myself and thought, 'With a name like Jamie he was probably a sales rep,' so I told my receptionist that he would have to wait. He did wait, and I am glad he did. It turned out that he was Jamie Thyer from The Worried Men. He said that my name was in his little black book as a tasty drummer and was I busy that night, as he had a gig and his drummer had let him down? Bearing in mind this was about 4.30 in the afternoon, I then asked, 'Where and what time to be there?' He said, '7.30 and at Bridgwater,' about 30 miles away from me! As it turned out I was available and agreed to play for them. I found the pub and when I went in there was a bass rig set up so I thought that I must be in the right place. The bass guitarist introduced himself to me, so I asked what sort of music we would be playing. He said very loud Rhythm and Blues – and he wasn't wrong! I ended up playing with the largest sticks I had but what a night! Jamie was a brilliant frontman, good on guitar and vocals and as mad as a hatter, but what a night!

Wishful Thinking, this was a duo that I used to jam with and occasionally would make their outfit into a trio with me on drums to play at larger functions.

Hot Dog Jackson with me on drums

With Steve White and Frank Aust from Hot Dog Jackson

Hot Dog Jackson, Frank Aust, the leader of Hot Dog Jackson, has become quite a friend over the years. Our bass guitarist suggested that he could help The Sneakers out one night when Billy was unavailable. Not only was he a tasty lead guitarist, but he was good on bass as well. The gig was at Happy Days Caravan Park Brean and since then he has helped us out quite a few

My Life with Music

times, on lead guitar mostly, and I have helped The Hot Dogs out on drums a few times. Whenever I watch them play I always get to sit in on the drums. For one night only we formed a band called Three of a Kind to help out Yeovil Labour Club when they were let down last-minute.

First Element, Shane was asked if he could dep with this band and he agreed, forgetting he had to go to South Wales that day. Rather than let the band down, he offered my services for the night. I didn't mind, but I knew very few of the songs that they played as most were self-written and very heavy – but I got away with it.

Tigress Sounds, this was a Butlins duo that got singers out of the audience and when they knew there was a drummer in the audience they snapped my arm off to play. The drummer Dave said to me that the Butlins organisation don't allow smoking on the stage (this was 1987) so when I need a fag and a pee I will call you up onstage. Well, this was the first day of our holiday and I ended up playing each lunchtime and evening that week!

The Echoes, I have played with them twice. They are a very good Bristol Rock'n'Roll band and I thoroughly enjoyed working with them.

The Fretmen, I have played for them three times. Roger McCourtney, their leader and lead guitarist, has played for and with me over the years. He is a very good lead guitarist.

The Honky-Tonks, I played with them three times and even helped them to get a regular drummer.

Howlin Dogs, once I sat in for my nephew as he was in hospital.
I played at many jam sessions and the odd festival, making lots of friends on

Paul Brimble

the way, many of whom I only knew by sight, but we had the same interest – music. Here are some photos of me playing at a festival at The Somerset Arms, Maiden Bradley.

Me jamming at a festival

Taffy introducing the next act

My Life with Music

Jamming with other musicians at a festival

Deep in thought

Paul Brimble

Some jam sessions

Line-up including John Williams and Geoff Collins

With like minded players

My Life with Music

the Sammy Milsom Jazz Band

Me playing the drums with the Sammy Milsom Jazz Band

I very often took bookings for the Sammy Milsom Jazz Band and one in particular was for a friend of mine, Roger Meadows. He wanted a trad band to play for his son's graduation from university; it was to be held at his house, which was enormous and had a swimming pool. The weather wasn't brilliant and because of the rain we had to play in the changing room but that didn't spoil the evening and many of the guests got wet anyway as they ended up in the swimming pool. The most unusual gig I arranged for the jazz band was for the ladies' circle. A totally female event, apart from the compère and the entertainment. It turned out that the Devizes Round Table who were supplying some male balloon dancers backed out and as a last resort two **male strippers** were hired. I was asked to put the music tapes on for both strippers: the first one went perfect but the second one snapped, and Ian Hobbs the compère asked if the band could play some music for the second stripper to get his clothes off. Sammy wasn't too happy with this but, as they say, 'the show must go on', so Sammy, Dave Beech and myself played some blues and the stripper finished his show. We were introduced by the compère as the 'eighth wonder of the world'! (Now, girls, I know what you get up to at these male stripper parties!) Sammy asked my wife if I could play the drums for him on Boxing Day one year. In those days I didn't play over Christmas as the children were still young but Sammy is hard to say no to. So she agreed with him: I would play. It turned out that the booking was at Sherborne, Dorset. The next thing was 'could I pick up the rest of the band and take them with me.' This meant that I left home at 4.00pm on Boxing Day and got home about 3.00am. You would think, "Oh well." But there was more to come! Sammy told us as we were approaching the hotel we won't get paid until he put a chitty in. I only **got my money in the middle of** February! I play over Christmas these days but with reservations.

With Tigris Sounds at Butlins Minehead

Me playing drums with Tigris Sounds at Butlins Minehead

My Life with Music

The Sneakers

The Sneakers: Paul, Chris, Billy, Dave

I HAVE BEEN PRIVILIGED TO HAVE WORKED WITH THE FOLLOWING:

Fred Wedlock ('the oldest swinger in town'). Spirelaine played with Fred on numerous occasions and I in particular got to know Fred quite well. We did a lot of charity gigs together and Fred turned round to me at Paulton Rovers Football Club one night and said, "Wouldn't it be nice to get paid?!" The last thing Fred ever did for me was to sign one of his CDs on his deathbed for a charity event that I had arranged for Ethan Smith, a very young boy that needed to go to America for a life-changing operation. My current band, The Sneakers, headlined the function and I went to Fred's funeral beforehand. I am sure Fred would be pleased that because of his, and others', input we were able to raise almost four thousand pounds on the night.

Paul Brimble

Acker Bilk and His Paramount Jazz Band. Spirelaine supported Acker and his band at Downside School, Stratton-on-the-Fosse, in their large hall. The event was for Dorothy House – a cancer hospice at Winsley near Bath. I was very impressed with Acker's attitude as, when you think, he only lives about seven miles away from the gig, so he could just turn up and play. But not Acker – he turned up at 5 o'clock and stayed until the end of the gig, allowing people to have photographs taken with him: he was a thoroughly nice person. The acoustics were not good for them and they didn't get the best sound, but that did not deter them from being one hundred percent professional. Since that night I called at Acker's bungalow in Pensford to ask for a signed CD as an auction item for the Ethan Smith appeal. Acker wasn't there but his wife took my details and I was asked to return so that Acker would sign a CD for me, and he also gave me some signed photos. The following week I brought Acker and his wife home from Fred Wedlock's funeral.

Adge Cutler and The Wurzels: The Decimal.5 supported Adge Cutler at the Frome Car Auctions back in 1971.

The Barron Knights: Spirelaine supported them in 1978 with a country band. The country band played the first set, Spirelaine second, Barron Knights third, and Spirelaine finished the night. How do you follow a band like The Barron Knights? We had a chat to their roadie and he said that if they were enjoying themselves they would do Johnny B. Goode as their final encore. I told the rest of our band that we should be in place on the stage behind them and when they finished we should carry on with the same song, which we did and we kept the crowd with us until the end of the show which didn't finish until 2.00am.

My Life with Music

Billy J. Kramer and the Dakotas. Spirelaine supported these at St Margaret's Hall, Bradford on Avon. There was a worry that they weren't going to show, as we were already set up and ready to go before they even turned up. The band came in a large coach and we couldn't see much for the smoke which was coming out of the exhaust pipe. Billy J. Kramer said that they had used more oil than diesel since they had left from Manchester. They were brilliant and played all of their hits and more.

The Wurzels. The Sneakers played with The Wurzels at Midsomer Norton cricket club. I must be one of the very few that has supported the original Adge Cutler and The Wurzels and also the current Wurzels. Not only that, I am a good friend of Kevin's from The Mangledwurzels, a Wurzels tribute act. The event at Midsomer Norton cricket club was spoiled by the sound engineers, so much so that when I spoke to Tommy Banner, their banjo player, at the end of our set he said that the monitored sound we were getting onstage was good. He thought that we had played well but when he heard the shite sound given to the audience he made up his mind to use their own PA system and refused to use the system that was already set up.

Ken Mackintosh. Spirelaine supported this great dance band twice, both times at the Assembly Rooms, Bath.

Joe Loss. Spirelaine supported him at the Assembly Rooms: he is without doubt one of the most arrogant people I have ever met. His band, however, were nice people and they did say that they got the best treatment and all the goodies by playing for Joe Loss.

Andy Ross. Spirelaine supported the Andy Ross Band at the time when they were resident band for *Come Dancing* on television. We actually helped to set up their PA system as their roadie couldn't get into the Assembly Rooms,

Paul Brimble

Bath. The caretaker had locked the doors and didn't open them again until a half an hour before the dance was due to start. Andy Ross was so pleased with us, he gave us each an LP of him and his band.

Jethro. Spirelaine played with him at Fosseway Country Club; he was not that funny. He had on a knitted jumper that reminded me of Dennis the Menace and no one could understand a word he said – mind you, this was a long time before he was famous.

Frank Carson. What a comedian! Spirelaine supported him at the Pavilion Bath. We were booked by the Post Office and they also booked a disc jockey. The event was to start at 7.30pm; a girl singer by the name of Helen Aserman asked us if she could sing a few songs with us and, as she had recently won the Fry Club 'Search for a Star' talent contest, we had no problem with that. At 7.20pm the room was empty, so the DJ who was supposed to start the show decided to have a shower and just then about five coaches turned up all at the same time. By 7.30pm the Pavilion was packed but no disco! We decided to start in his place and tried all types of music before the crowd hit onto the 60s and that was then the theme for the rest of the night: the disco got unloaded with its 80s music and reloaded with the 60s.
Frank came in and introduced himself to us: he was a perfect gentleman and he rattled off joke after joke. Brilliant!

Leslie Crowther. I had a phone call from the Frome Enterprise Centre on the Marston Trading Estate asking if Spirelaine would play at their premises. It was a function for physically and mentally impaired adults and children from the Frome and District area. I immediately said 'Yes' and that we would play for nothing. I was told that I must charge, even if it was just expenses, as they felt they couldn't approach us to play again if we didn't get paid. In the end grudgingly I agreed expenses only. I think we got a fiver each

My Life with Music

and that was paid by a local businessman, so we didn't feel too bad. Leslie Crowther who, by the way, was their president, also attended the evening and what a man! He won at least five major prizes in the raffle, only to give them away to the residents. I am talking a television, bike and a full-size teddy bear amongst other prizes. I sat next to Leslie for our refreshments and he told me all about his drinking problem and how the press hounded him. He said in joking way that his wife was the drinker in his home and with a wink he said to me, 'You will have to guess what is in this glass.' We played the same event again the following year and he invited us to his house to have a musical evening with him, but sadly we never got round to it and then he had the serious car accident.

Humphrey Lyttelton. The Decimal.5 supported Humphrey Lyttelton at the Bath and West Showground. It was advertised as a Trad Jazz Evening and we employed a clarinet and trombone player for the night. I don't know what Humphrey knew about it being a trad night as he brought a modern jazz band featuring Kathy Stobart on tenor sax. They went down like a lead balloon and we had to finish the evening as they were booed off.

Tank Sherman. The Sneakers were part of a cabaret evening with Tank and a girl singer; we let him use our PA system and he was so grateful that he gave us a CD and a video each. At the time he was a very fat comedian. In 2009 I was on holiday at Devon Cliffs Sandy Bay and Tank was the evening cabaret on the Sunday night. I had a job to recognise him he had lost so much weight (he had a gastric band). He recognised me and even recalled where he had worked with us – again he gave me his up-to-date CD and video. He also rated The Sneakers, saying that they were one of the best versatile bands he had worked with.

TANK SHERMAN

Tank Sherman

Adrian Varcoe. The Decimal.5 supported Adrian, a well-known female impersonator, at Arnos Court Hotel, Bristol.

Dave Wolfe. A well-known comedian in the 80s was booked to play at Coleford British Legion and Spirelaine were to support him. The only problem was that he went to Coleford in the Forest of Dean by mistake and to say that he had lost his sense of humour by the time he arrived at the right venue would be the case. We had already started by the time he got there and a message was sent up to us asking if we could play him on with the 'Parkinson' theme and that was agreed. His act was brilliant, but when we got to chat with him later he was not a happy bunny – but, as he said, 'the show must go on'.

My Life with Music

Iris Williams. Don Moss, who was the presenter of *Mr and Mrs*, a television show on HTV, saw Spirelaine at the Fosseway Country Club when he was guest speaker for the Lions and said he would like to book them up. It was about a week later that I had a phone call from Don on my office phone and, thinking someone was taking the Mick, nearly put the phone down on him. I am glad I didn't, because he offered me a slot supporting Iris Williams (she had a no. 1 hit with 'He Was Beautiful') at the Bristol Wine Festival.

The Rubettes. The Decimal.5 supported The Rubettes at the Winter Gardens Weston-super-Mare. I have since met Paul Da Vinci, the lead vocalist credited with singing their number one hit, 'Sugar Baby Love'.

The Band of the Royal Marines. Spirelaine were booked to play a two-nighter at The Pavilions Plymouth for the South West of England Rotary Conference. We were to play on the Friday evening backing the Frome Old Tyme Musical Group (some of The Woodlanders and some of the Beckington Players). We finished the night with all types of music for the dancers. On the Saturday the Pipes and Bugle Band of the Royal Marines played, doing their very polished routines, and after this we shared the dance music with the Band of the Royal Marines for the rest of the evening.

Alan Moore (local singer/guitarist also an actor on *Coronation Street*). Alan Moore was probably the first local popstar we ever had. He had a band called 'The Blue Jean Set' and I was asked if I could play the drums for him, as he was playing a gig for the Cliff Richard Tearfund and he thought the drums would beef up the sound. Dave Stock was already booked to play and had also done the same gig a year previously, so I had no hesitation to do it – apart from the fact that I had already paid to watch the show (talk about pay to play). I even got to play my washboard as well. The night was good, even though Alan was changing everything about! It didn't matter much to me as

Paul Brimble

I wasn't at any of the practices. At the end of the evening, on the way home, I had the trailer detach from the car going down Kilmersdon Hill and it did a bit of damage to a set of railings at the bottom of the hill and also some slight damage to my kit.

Rock 'n' Roll reunion

Rock'n'Roll reunion: Bill Bolton. Mary Attwood. Paul Brimble. Dave Stock. Janet Tanner. Ken Eades. Alan Moore.

Colin Coombes. Colin sang a few songs with us at the Riviera Hotel Torquay, but he has been a good mate to The Sneakers by letting us set up our kit at Haydon Que Club. He is well known for his fundraising nights for the Flying Ambulance Appeal and has over the years collected a lot of money for them.

My Life with Music

LOCAL BANDS

Bernard Emm and the Rythmairs

The Don Webb Band

Ron Lamb and the Masqueraders

The Saxtones

Johnny, Mike & The Shades

The Ramrods

The Midrod Ends

The Firebrands

Eddy Dark and The Salvos

Dave and the Druids

Rocking Olly and The Boys

The Creatures

The Hermits

The Decimal.5

The Robins

Aubergene

Starlites

Spotlights

Just Uss

Scorpio

Sting

Sirocco

Lot 39

Reflected Number

Bee Jays

Sammy Milsom

Neon Rainbeaux

Bitter Greene

Ray Starr

Concordians

Just Mckay

Riverside Showband

Raffia

Alpha

Atlantis

Chris Reeves

Len James Dance Band

Back Tracking

Klass

Merry Macs

Tim May Set

The Deckchairs

Pentworth People

Sandy's People

Rockin Horse

Kelly

Superfly

Truth

Lady Blue

Cirrus

The Marriners

These are the bands I remember.

Paul Brimble

The drum kits I have had during my career

1962 not sure of the make – proper old-fashioned with skulls and loops, also pig skin heads on all the drums

1965 Gigster blue sparkle with matching bass drum snare drum and bongos

1967 added white Olympic hanging tom and floor tom

1972 purchased Beverley four-drum grey oyster kit

1973 Spirelaine with the Beverley kit

Spirelaine playing Wells Mendip Ballroom

1974 bought chrome Tama Five drum kit

Richard and me at the Masons Arms Frome

1976 bought Pearl double bass drum twelve drum kit in black fibre

LOOKING SHARP: Local band Spirelaine, featuring Paul and Dave Stocks, Richard Doughty and Kim Hyde, played a concert at Frome Theatre this week in 1976

Spirelaine featuring my twelve-piece Pearl kit

1979 bought Ludwig Tequila Sunrise John Bonham kit

Ludwig John Bonham Vistalite kit

1993 bought a wine-coloured Pearl Export kit.

Pearl eleven-piece

1994 bought a red Ludwig kit.

Dave Seward, me, Dan Seward and Simon Carder

1998 bought a silver Pearl Export kit.

Pearl five-piece

1998 bought two silver Pearl Export kits, one for my son's 18th birthday, the other for me, and in 1999 made up a double bass drum kit for myself.

Eight-piece Pearl kit

Twenty-inch bass drum silver Pearl Export kit to add to the other Pearl kit, making it an eleven-piece kit

Ludwig Jellybean Vistalite eight-piece kit

Ludwig Jellybean

DW, PDP seven-piece white kit

Dw. Pdp. seven-piece

My Life with Music

CHANGING STYLES

When Alan Braithwaite and Billy Colvin helped me out at the Bodkin House wedding I didn't realise what a change would eventually happen to me regarding music. Up until now, I had been reasonably happy with Spirelaine, the band that I had formed way back in 1973 but I had now caught the 60s bug and was playing the music that I had started playing when I was still at school. Alan's party piece was an extended version of Dire Straits' 'Sultans of Swing', so we decided to call ourselves The Sultans.

Alan and Billy were committed to Backbeat, a Beatles tribute band, so when I got enquiries for gigs I had to find out if they were available before taking the bookings but, bearing in mind I was still running Spirelaine, we still managed to play most of the gigs available.

Billy is a guitar teacher and he is the best bass player I have ever played with. He was always busy depping with other bands besides Backbeat and The Sultans. One band, Saffron, tried their hardest to poach him, but as he was busy with The Sultans and stayed committed to Backbeat, he declined the offer. Alan was less committed and was happy to take any bookings I could offer him.

The Sultans did the wedding bookings and I managed with a couple of contacts to get us bookings at Stratton British Legion and at the Fir Tree, Writhlington. We built up a good following, and one night Spirelaine had a booking at Yeovil Labour Club. It was our first time at this club: a good friend of ours, a brilliant lead guitarist by the name of Roger McCourtney, got Spirelaine three bookings and he was to play with us on these gigs. Well, the first booking turned into a right nightmare. Kim had problems with his rotary cabinet and played so loud Roger couldn't be heard. We ended up having a row. Roger, who was completely innocent of any wrongdoing, said that we would have to play the other two gigs without him.

I gave great thought to the situation and asked Shaun, the entertainments manager, if I could swap Spirelaine out with The Sultans, and he was more than happy to oblige. This turned out to be a milestone in my career. One night, as I was driving to the Yeovil Labour Club, I got a phone call to say that Alan wasn't coming that night but that his mate would help us out! You can only imagine what I felt at the time, but at least Alan had arranged cover for the night and, as it turned out, I had played with this guitarist before: his name was C.J. and he had helped Spirelaine out at Farrington Golf Club one time and he was very good.

Paul Brimble, Billy Colvin, Alan Braithwaite

The Sultans setting up with Alan Braithwaite

Billy was quite happy because, unlike Alan who was a very good guitarist, C.J. could also sing: which meant they were able to share the vocals. We went down a storm that night and in the audience there was a talent scout for a club in Weymouth and he asked if we would like to play for them. I explained that C.J. was only helping us out for the night, but he said that he wanted the line-up that he had just seen. So I agreed, and took the booking. I decided to form another band with C.J. and Billy and called it The Sneakers, which is a name from a band that C.J. had previously been in.

My Life with Music

Alan eventually got fed up and gave up playing, but not until we had played at a few pubs and clubs. The Sultans played at Bodkin House, Cumberwell Golf Club, The Fir Tree, Stratton Legion, Prattens Social Club, The Anchor Warminster, Yeovil Labour Club and The King William IV, Combe Down, Bath.

C.J. had joined up with me using the names of The Sultans and The Sneakers. Under the name of The Sneakers when Billy wasn't available we used a bass guitarist by the name of Tony Paul, a very tasty bass player with a very good pedigree. I met him when he was working with my son Shane making circuit boards. I then went on to play with him in the Pat Mallon Big Country Band and he also was bass guitarist with the very well-known 'Old Man's Hat' blues band. Tony also played for a short while with Close to the Wire and eventually joined Sirroco, where he stayed until they broke up some five years or more later. I actually put his name forward to Sirocco after their bass player, Roy Bracey, was killed in a road accident.

Me, C.J. and Tony played The Anchor in Warminster and also The King William IV at Combe Down, Bath. I also played with Tony in the Pat Mallon Big Country Band as far afield as Cinderford and Bridgwater, and with us were Roger McCourtney and Dave Stock.

I was getting more and more disillusioned with the Spirelaine gigs: they lacked spark. I was always telling Dave Stock about the good nights I was having playing 60s Rock'n'Roll and he asked if he could come with me one night. I took him to Yeovil Labour Club: he was blown away and we got him up to sing a couple of songs and he loved it – so did the crowd and before long, we got him to bring his guitar. It wasn't long before he was asked to join the band, albeit on a system whereby if the bookers can afford the price of a four-piece band, and if not Dave would stand down. I still ran Spirelaine and did so for more years to come: the last booking was New Year's Eve 2004.

Tony Paul

Tony Paul

Me, C.J. and Tony

C.J., me and Tony

When it was our 25th wedding anniversary my eldest son Charlie gave us a holiday as a present in a hotel at Torquay, and while we were there I noticed a poster advertising Chantilly Lace, a band that Spirelaine had beaten in a talent contest in Bristol. I asked the proprietor if they had live music at the hotel: I explained that I played in a band and that I would love to play in their hotel. I didn't expect the answer I got, because he said that he had a free weekend in November, and if I wanted it, it was mine. I rang the band up and they were all up for it; I explained that the only guarantee I could give them was that we would get a free bed, breakfast and evening meal weekend for us all and our partners, and didn't know if we would get any money.

We looked forward to this venture: it was not very full on that weekend, but we have done two weekends every year since, sometimes three. Also we have done two New Year's Eve three-nighters in another hotel at Torquay. When I was offered the Torquay gigs the only card I had in my pocket was for The Sultans and that was the name we were booked under. As the years have gone on we have managed to get the name changed to The Sneakers as the name for the band. We have built up a good following for these weekends and often sell every room.

We also did two charity functions for two young boys with cerebral palsy and both were very successful and raised a lot of money.

Me, with Henry Ford – one of the young boys that we did a charity function for

Me with Henry Ford

Paul Brimble

I held my 60th birthday party at Mardons, as did Billy his 50th. Here are some photos:

Steve White (the old man) from Old Man's Hat.

Me with Steve White

Ken Jones, Brian Smalley, both from Neon Rainbeaux

Brian Smalley and friends singing 'Mustang Sally'

My Life with Music

Billy Colvin, Shane Brimble, Adrian (Charlie) Brimble

Billy, Shane and Charlie

My grandson Jaydon singing 'Teenage Kicks'

My grandson Jaydon

This is my life through the eyes of Mrs Brimble at my 60th birthday party

This Is Your Life *as told to me by my wife Mary*

Frank Aust from Hot Dog Jackson

Frank and Kath

My Life with Music

VENUES

Colerne Constitutional Club: I first played here 40-odd years ago, and was asked about eight years ago if I would like to play here again with The Sneakers. We even had Russell Crook, the bass guitarist from The Wurzels, turn up in the audience one evening.

High Wycombe, the Irish Club: The Sneakers did a weekender here. We played the Saturday night and the Sunday afternoon and were looked after very well by our host: many thanks, Dave.

Bute Court Hotel, Torquay: At least twice a year The Sneakers play a three-night weekend at the Bute: more often than not it is a sell-out.

Bishops Court Hotel, Torquay. Part-owned by Neil, the owner of the Bute Hotel Torquay.

Haydon Que Club: I play the Que Club normally twice a year and have done for many years.

Frome Masonic Hall: Another venue where I have played with numerous bands.

Hotel Prince Regent, Weymouth: A very prestigious venue. I have played here with The Sneakers many times.

Warminster Conservative Club: The Sneakers supported Tank Sherman here in cabaret.

Waterside Holiday Park: Bowleaze Cove, Weymouth. This is as good as it gets: the lights, the crowd and the excitement. What a venue: The Sneakers play here twice a year on average. We got this gig after a fan of ours from Peasedown St John that had a caravan at Waterside told the management, "You've got to get The Sneakers down here, they are better than the bands that you book." The rest is history: we went down a storm and have played here for five years or more. Many thanks to Nobby Collins.

Happy Days Caravan Park Brean: The Sneakers played here twice and on one of these bookings we used Frank Aust on bass.

Midsomer Norton Rugby Club: I have played here with three different bands.

Prattens Social Club, Midsomer Norton: I was with Spirelaine, The Sultans and The Sneakers here.

Wyke Regis Working Men's Club: One of the clubs I can honestly say I look forward to playing at. We always have a good night. I wish we could get more bookings each year, but when I suggested four I was told that most bands only get two – so I shut up.

Radstock Working Men's Club: I have played here for many years for many different bands.

Welton Rovers Football Club: Another club that I have played in with many other bands and I have held some good parties here for my family and musician friends. I now play for the Midsomer Norton Community Trust first Thursday afternoon function about three times a year.

Continue Forms: I suppose you could now include The Sneakers as a 'corporate act' – as we played in a marquee on the factory premises to celebrate their 30 years in business.

My Life with Music

Buckland Dinham Beer Festival: What a joke: this must be the worst festival The Sneakers has ever played at. I don't know where the organisers got the sound engineer from but he was rubbish; what with that and the lack of people (mind you, according to our local paper there were thousands) and the weather I don't think we will be playing there again.

Frys Club: This is a club that I have played with many bands, it was a real pain to get our gear into as it was upstairs and then a route march halfway back into the building (no fun when you have to take in a Hammond organ and a rotary speaker). The club has now got a new venue, it is named the Fry Pavilion and we play there for the Fry Rock'n'Roll club usually once a year and sometimes twice. I get on very well with Dave Bateman the organiser: he reckons I am an inspiration because of how I have got over my stroke and heart problems.

Wells Buses Club: This club has a bad habit of booking you up and then cancelling for private bookings.

Bath University: I only played here once and it was with The Sneakers; we played for a Masonic dinner dance.

The Dolphin Ilchester: The Sneakers played twice for Stan's big birthday parties. Stan is Billy's brother-in-law.

Bridgwater Sports and Social Club: The Sneakers played here twice for Leroc. Obviously our timing was good. It was great to see the dance floor full all night.

Paul Brimble

Weymouth Pavilion: The Sneakers played with The Bristol Comets here and it was a brilliant night. I had met most of them before and it was great to work with them.

The Bristol Comets

The Bristol Comets

Weymouth Working Men's Club: This club is on the harbour in Weymouth: it was always a good night. The Sneakers, they say, are the most popular band that plays there. It is always full, but that could be down to the bingo.

Farmborough village hall: The last time I played here was with The Sneakers and it was for Farmborough School. We had a brilliant night. Again, it is a hall that I have played with many bands.

My Life with Music

Conygre Hall Timsbury: Another hall that is good to play in. It has a large stage and the hall has very good acoustics. I have played with many bands here.

Doulting Village Hall: I have played here twice, both times with different bands.

Charlton Kings Club, Cheltenham: A long way to go but the crowd love The Sneakers.

Wells Golf Club: I have played here twice with two different bands.

Bedminster Down Ex-Service Club: Only played here twice and The Sneakers managed to get Roger McCourtney to play for us once, as C.J. was ill. I would love to play here again but it is an agency club and we don't really use agents.

Pump Room, Bath: Crap acoustics whatever band you are with and I have played here with three.

Frome Town Football Club: Nice club, good sound: The Sneakers did a cancer charity dance here and Spirelaine played here regularly over the years.

Webbington Country Club: The Sneakers played here twice, both times for the Jaguar Car Club. Frank Aust played lead guitar on the second one, in place of C.J., who had a mouth ulcer.

Riviera Hotel, Bowleaze Cove, Weymouth: The Sneakers played for the Leroc dancing weekend: it was very well organised.

The Sneakers

Wyke Regis Social Club: One of the best working men's clubs that The Sneakers play. It is a large club and we get a very good following. I always look forward to playing here.

TROUBLE AT GIGS

There haven't been many gigs where fights and arguments have occurred but there have been a few. Back in 1976 Spirelaine were playing in the Masonic Hall in Frome and this young man started to chat Mary up. This was long before we were married. It didn't upset me too much until he kept on and it was obvious she was getting very upset with him. I don't know what got into me, but I stopped playing midway through a song and sorted him out – then went on to complete the evening's entertainment.

In the same year Spirelaine were playing at the Midsomer Norton Community Centre and fighting broke out. We stopped playing and Richard, our bass player, announced that, if they didn't stop fighting, we would pack up and go home. Some of Midsomer Norton's hardest cases were there that evening. I hid behind my drums expecting the worst, but to my amazement the fight stopped and again we carried on for the rest of the night.

The Sneakers played at Codford. When a fight broke out luckily for us it was at the end of the evening and we finished about ten minutes early.

NEW YEAR'S EVE BOOKINGS

1973 **Wells EMI:** this was the first year that Spirelaine was formed I took the booking using our normal Saturday rates, not realising that we could get three times the price for New Year's Eve.

1974 **Coleford British Legion**

1975 **Bath Century House:** Spirelaine only played this venue the once and had a brilliant night.

1976 **Farrington Village Hall:** This was the original hall and Spirelaine went on to play many gigs there. Even though the hall was an old building of timber construction the acoustics were very good. Pity the same couldn't be said of the heating!

1977 **Midsomer Norton Community Centre:** This venue is no longer there; Spirelaine played there numerous times with a lot of stories to tell, mostly about fighting and trouble etc. We had some really good nights there but the times that we got to play right up to the agreed finishing times were few and far between because of trouble.

1978 **Coleford British Legion.**

1979 **Coleford British Legion:** Probably the hall that I have played the most New Year's Eve gigs at over my playing career with various bands. This particular year could have been a disaster but for a friend of mine having a four wheel-drive truck and took our kit to the venue as the snow was nine inches deep. We had a capacity crowd as no one could get out of the village. Our keyboard player didn't get there but we managed to play the gig.

1980 Coleford **British Legion**

1981 **Paulton Rovers:** People were outside from 6.30pm waiting to get in for an 8.30pm start!

1982 **Paulton Rovers**

1983 **Westbury Labour Club:** My wife was pregnant and having a bad time. The band had been to the club in the morning to set up for the night and when I got home my wife said that she didn't feel well enough to go out that night. I rang Dave Burfoot, our singer, and told him I would drive him to the gig so that he could have a drink; when I picked him up at 7.00pm he had drunk a bottle of gin and was drunk. We had to fill him up with black coffee all night and I really gave him some stick but lucky for us, we got through the night!

1984 **Paulton Rovers** 1985 Coleford British Legion 1986 Paulton Rovers

---

1987 **Westbury Blue Circle**

1988 **Frome Town**

1989 **Westbury Blue Circle**

1990 **Coleford British Legion**

My Life with Music

1991 **Coleford British Legion**

1992 **Frome Town Football Club**

1993 **Kilmersdon Village Hall**

1994 **Coleford British Legion**

1995 **Stratton British Legion**

1996 **Camerton Village Hall**

1997 **Camerton Village Hall** (for Fosseway Bowls Club)

1998 **Westbury Blue Circle**

1999 **Westbury Laverton Institute:** This was to be the best-paid gig ever as it was the Millennium booking and as bands would be wanted for all types of organisations we would all be able to charge extortionate rates. An agent in Bristol offered me a booking for £4700. I asked: what was the chance of this booking taking place? His response was, "If you throw enough against the wall some will stick." I decided to decline that booking. I did, however, get a phone call from Westbury Rotary Club enquiring for that Millennium booking. I told them the price that I thought was fair for that night and we came up with a compromise that suited us. I nearly wasn't able to play the gig as I had a mild heart attack just days before, on Christmas Day but, as they say, 'the show must go on'.

2000 No Booking, I spent the night with my next-door neighbours Ted and Jean.

Paul Brimble

2001 **Stratton British Legion**

2002 **Stratton British Legion**

2003 **Midsomer Norton Cricket Club**

2004 **Timsbury Conygre Hall:** this was Spirelaine's last booking.

2005 **Bishops Court Hotel Torquay**

2006 **Centenary Club Weymouth:** This was a good night but for some indifference from a couple of people on the club committee. They tried to make our wives pay to see us. I feel very strongly about this – our wives give up a lot for our musical commitments and hardly ever get to socialise with us because we are normally working. I went as far as telling the people concerned that if they insisted on our wives having to pay I would take our kit down and go home, and that they could go and tell the hundred or so people waiting outside what had happened. Obviously they declined; and a good night was enjoyed by all.

2007 **Bishops Court Hotel Torquay:** This was an unusual gig as it was to be played over three nights. I took the booking as I thought it would be nice to leave the equipment set up for the three nights. As it turned out we had to play in two separate rooms and had to set up twice, but I must admit the money was good.

2008 **Mardons Social Club:** This was a brilliant gig and it was the first time that the Mardons crowd got to see and hear Billy Colvin in full Highland dress and playing the bagpipes.

My Life with Music

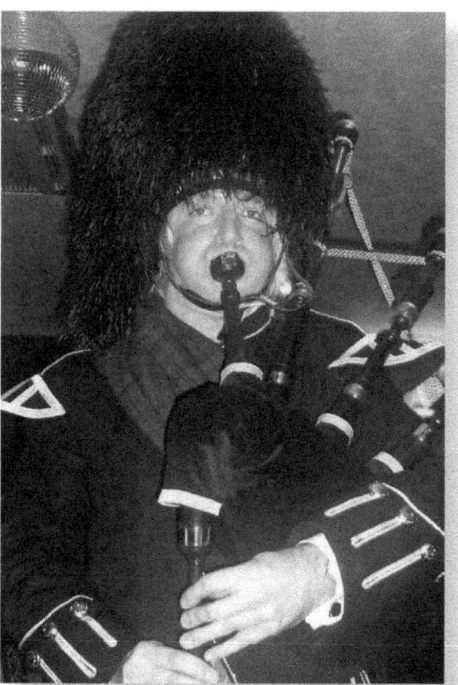

Billy playing the bagpipes

2009 Mardons Social Club: A virtual sell-out, The Sneakers ended up doing the best part of a five-hour gig complete with Billy Colvin playing the bagpipes in full Highland dress at midnight.

2010 Mardons Social Club: Brilliant night, all tickets sold before the event. Dave Stock started the evening playing lead guitar to Shadows backing tracks. The Sneakers then played a couple of sets before midnight, and Billy Colvin then came into the room dressed in full Highland dress playing the bagpipes! After Auld Lang Syne we played virtually non-stop until ten past one and the crowd loved it.

Paul Brimble

2011 **Coleford Royal British Legion:** This is one gig I will never forget, as I didn't get to play it! The reason being that I ended up in the Royal United Hospital with a stroke. I set my drums up at 9.00 in the morning but I had a numb sensation in my right hand, more the wrist area – but managed to play a couple of songs and convinced myself and the others that I would be able to manage the gig. On the way home from setting up I called into the chemist's for a bit of advice and was told to go to Paulton Hospital and see a doctor. The outcome was me being sent to the Royal United Hospital in Bath, where I stayed for hours – and missed the gig. Luckily I had put my son on standby: he did the gig for me and by all accounts did a brilliant job. This gig appeared to be my swansong as for the next eight months I was hampered with ongoing bad health, including ten admissions to hospital. I had my heart stopped and started twice (a procedure called a cardioversion); also I had a chemical-induced cardioversion. I had three echo procedures (where a camera is put down the throat to look for possible blood clots) and an angiogram (fortunately I didn't need a stent). I had three ablation operations in the Bristol Heart Hospital, all of which failed, and then I was fitted with a pacemaker which, after the first six weeks' check, was deemed a success.

**

LIFE AFTER MY STROKE

My book was due to be completed at this point but unfortunately for me, the night before New Year's Eve 2011, when I went to bed I was leaving the bathroom pulling the light switch, and couldn't find it so proceeded to use my other hand (I didn't realise I had lost some of the use of my right hand) to turn the light off.

I got up early the following morning and drove over to Coleford British Legion, setting up our equipment for our New Year's Eve gig. I asked the others to play three songs with me, as I was a bit concerned about the strange feeling I had in my wrist and I seemed to manage alright. I said goodbye to the others and proceeded to go home.

As I was driving through Midsomer Norton I decided to call into the chemist's to see if there was anything that could be done about my wrist and was advised to visit Paulton Hospital, where I would be seen by a doctor.

I was first seen by a triage nurse. She was going to send me home with some painkillers, but had spoken to the doctor who insisted on seeing me before I left to go home. The doctor put a device on the end of my finger and asked how long had I had an irregular heartbeat. I said that I didn't know I had one, but told him that I was being treated for angina. The doctor said that I had an AF of 170, which was like talking to me in Japanese, and then said that as we were going into a three-day Bank Holiday he didn't want me on his conscience and would I be happy if he spoke to the RUH in Bath about me? – and that is what he did.

The Casualty Department at the RUH said for me to go in asap – and in the meantime the doctor told me that he thought that I had had a stroke. I went home and had some lunch and told my wife that I had to go to the RUH to have my hand seen to. It wasn't until we were almost at the hospital that I told her the doctor had thought I had suffered a stroke. My wife nearly drove through the hedge!

When I arrived at the Casualty Department they were waiting for me and put me straight into a wheelchair and within minutes I was all gowned up and had an ECG, heart scan, brain scan and chest X-ray all in about an hour. After I kept on and on that I had a gig to get to that evening I was told that I would be lucky if I was to go home in less than 48 hours.

What was I to do? I had never let anyone down in 50 years of drumming, not even when I had gangrenous appendicitis. I was able to get cover for all of my gigs. As luck would have it, my youngest son Shane, who is a brilliant drummer, was available and did the gig for me and, from the comments I received, did a very good job.

Paul Brimble

I was told by my Casualty doctor that, had I played that gig instead of going to hospital, I would have almost certainly died on the stage that night – so at least I live to tell the tale!

That was the beginning of eight months of uncertainty as to whether I was to ever play the drums again, let alone be a regular drummer in my own band!

I asked my doctor how many days there were in a month and his reply was it depended on which month it was! I explained that the reason that I needed to know was that I was not allowed to drive for a month, but that I had a gig on the 28th of January which would be 28 days after my stroke, and I needed to tow the band gear to Yeovil Labour Club that night with my car and trailer. The doctor thought for a minute and then asked me some questions relevant to my general health and said that as far as he was concerned there were 28 days in every month!! And gave me permission to drive.

The gig at Yeovil Labour Club I decided was too much, and too soon, for me to play the whole night so I found another drummer, Mike Goodliffe, to help me out. I set up my drums and asked Mike to play the first half and when it was about twenty minutes from the break I took over the drums and Cherry picked five or six show-off songs including 'Wipe Out' – much to my wife's disgust!

During the break I told Mike that the rest of the evening was now his, and as he had never rehearsed with the band before, he did an excellent job. A couple of weeks later I felt well enough to attempt a full night, but under my wife's insistence asked my son to be there in case I was unable to complete the night. Shane did play a few songs, but was not really needed on the night. About 3 o'clock in the morning I had a serious atrial fibrillation attack and was rushed by ambulance to the RUH and was kept in for a few days.

It became obvious that The Sneakers would have to use dep drummers for a while as I was quite seriously ill, and there didn't seem to be any light at the end of the tunnel. That year I was in hospital for every Bank Holiday except August. This was a turning point as it marked my return to the band.

My Life with Music

For my comeback eight months later, we had two gigs booked in Weymouth – on the Friday, Chesil Vista Holiday Park, and on the Saturday, Wyke Regis Working Men's. I played both and felt quite well but tired; the rest of the band kept an eye on me, showing their concern for my welfare, asking me every ten minutes or so as to how I was feeling.

I was very concerned that there was only one booking taken for the following year and soon started looking for work for the band. I had some success: I managed to pull in 28 bookings that week by ringing a few of my contacts, but bearing in mind I normally had a healthy diary by the end of July for the following year, I think I did quite well.

Since 2003 the band did three night bookings at various hotels in Torquay, normally twice a year but sometimes we did three. The year that I was ill we didn't have any booked as the Bute Court Hotel went into receivership. Lots of our regular followers kept on to me asking would we ever play Torquay again.

I decided to canvas the hotels in Torquay and booked a weekend away in November staying at the Rainbow Hotel Torquay, and took Dave, another member of the band, with me and both of our wives. I was armed with a letter of introduction, a CD and DVD of live gigs and proceeded to visit all the hotels on the Belgrave Road – with not a lot of success, but it had to be done.

A couple of days later after we were home, I received a phone call from a lady by the name of Kate who over the years I have got to know quite well. She had read my introduction letter and watched the DVD and was very interested in what we had to offer. She agreed my terms and gave me a three-day weekend of which we, as a band, pushed out as much information as we could. We even arranged a coach from our local area. The weekend was a great success and we were given another weekend for the following November. We have done two weekends each year since, with all being complete sell-outs.

Marco, the owner of The Rainbow, talked to me about the possibility of playing New Year's Eve. I spoke to the rest of the band and offered our services for another three-nighter. Our conditions were met and it turned out to be really good. Bearing in mind this was a **new** audience to us, it was a brilliant three-nighter!

I received a phone call from a man named Geoff Rogers saying he owned a hotel in Dawlish and The Sneakers had been recommended to him. He agreed a price with me and we turned up to play at his hotel's loyalty weekend.

We were greeted at the reception by his daughter Louise. She said, "I suppose you are the band, follow me." She proceeded to take us into a very large ballroom, saying, "This is where the good bands play, but you will be playing in there." Pointing to a much smaller room!

We went into the reception area again and looked at the advertising board and saw the advert for us. This read: "The Sneakers are new to the Langstone Cliff Hotel and we are assured that they will fit like a glove, but if they don't we will tell you who recommended them."

We were beginning to feel a bit anxious and then a bit later in the evening I was invited into the main office and told we would be having an early night. I asked why and was told that the audience was rubbish and all the other bands that they had were finished by 10.30–11.00-ish. I didn't want to get into an argument but I told him I was 'old school' and that there wasn't such a thing as a rubbish audience, but that there is such a thing as 'rubbish entertainment'. I asked what time we were booked to finish and was told midnight.

We were told that we had to start at 9.00pm, even though the guests were only on their second course. So we did some light music that they could listen to whilst they were still eating and we kept our eye on when they were ready to dance. We then proceeded to give them what they wanted – the outcome was that we finished at 12.30am, and that was only because it would be unfair to other guests in the hotel.

By 9.00am the following morning I had an e-mail from the hotel thanking us for our performance and more bookings! We are now regulars at the

My Life with Music

Langstone Cliff Hotel Dawlish.

I am now finishing my book and I hope it made for good reading. It is my wish to carry on drumming until I am unable. I would like to thank all of the people who have made my career in music so enjoyable. That includes our devoted followers, bookers, clubs, hotels, anywhere that I have been privileged to play. Most important – my lovely wife Mary not only for allowing me to follow my vocation, but also for actively encouraging me and for nursing me through my illness.

This was to be the end of my book but I seem to have had a second wind to my life and with my music, and I have decided to include the next five years or so as they have an interesting outcome to me.

It took eight months before I was fit to play the drums again, albeit I tried a couple of times, once at Yeovil Labour Club a month after I had my stroke. It was the first time I was officially allowed to drive and The Sneakers had arranged for Mike Goodliffe to play the drums, but I was to tow the trailer with all the band kit to the gig and to play as many songs as I thought I could cope with, and played the last six songs in the first half, finishing with 'Wipe Out', much to my wife's disgust as she thought I should not have done it as it is such a demanding number. After the break I gave the drumsticks to Mike and told him, "The rest of the night is yours."

The following week I played at Midsomer Norton Social Club with my son Shane there to take over if I was taken ill or couldn't manage to complete the night; he wasn't needed but I let him do a few numbers. Early the following morning I was rushed to hospital again and I didn't play again until August Bank Holiday weekend where I played two gigs at Weymouth. The first on the Friday was at Chesil Vista Holiday Park, and Saturday at Wyke Regis Working Men's Club. Both gigs went well. I was a bit tired but very pleased. I had to see my surgeon Mr Ed Duncan from the BRI in Bristol for my discharge from his care: he was quite happy with me. I gave him a video of my first weekend back playing proper: he said this was gold dust for him, as people who are fitted with pacemakers want to know their limitations as to what they can do! I can now add drums to swimming, running etc etc!

2012 was very busy for The Sneakers, as it was The Queen's Diamond Jubilee Year. The band used some very good drummers to take my place and didn't let any customers down. I went from strength to strength but was worried about 2013, as at this time of the year (September) there was only one booking for the next year in the diary. Because of how ill I had been I think they were scared to think the worst, but were hesitant to take any bookings in case they were all to join other bands or form another band without me, and didn't want to think about the latter.

I decided to do a chase on my regular clubs and venues and managed to pick up 28 gigs for the next year. The Torquay 60s weekends that we had been playing since 2003 had dried up because the Bute Court Hotel had gone bankrupt at the beginning of 2012 and we thought that was an end of an era.

I took Mary, Dave and Elaine to Torquay for a Tinsel and Turkey weekend and we stayed at the Rainbow International Hotel which is opposite the Bute Court Hotel. Armed with a DVD a CD and a letter of introduction regarding The Sneakers and what we were able to offer, I canvassed all the hotels in Belgrave Road and when we arrived home awaited the results.

I didn't have to wait long as at the end of that week I received a call from a lady named Kate and, surprise, surprise, it was from the Rainbow International Hotel where we had stayed the previous week. After we spoke about the band she took me on face value and offered us a three-day weekend the following April (2013) and she agreed my terms and conditions, namely rooms for us and our partners, bed, breakfast and evening meals and a fixed fee for entertaining.

The 60s weekend went well and the hotel was pretty full. Kate was so pleased that she offered us the same deal for the following November and we were to do this as a 60s Tinsel and Turkey with Billy, our bass player, to play the bagpipes on the imaginary New Year's Eve. Needless to say it went down well and we were booked for the following May and November, and both of these were completely sold out!

At the May weekend I had a chat with Marco, the owner of the Rainbow, about the possibility of The Sneakers to play New Year's Eve and it was agreed that we would play the 30th and 31st December and 1st January for a fee mutually agreed between us with our usual conditions, and this also was a sell-out!

The Sneakers had played at Torquay over the New Year's Eve period twice before with both times being at the Bishops Court Hotel. The last three months of 2012 were a bit of a challenge for me as I was always wondering if my heart problems would come back. My fellow musicians in the band were always looking to me for reassurance as to how I was feeling health-wise and were bringing my kit in for me.

My wife insisted that I get rid of the trailer and get a van. I located a Renault Trafic seven-seater which I had the windows blacked out and inside had it transformed into a crew bus by having two rows of three seats (one row behind the driver) and a timber bulkhead to keep the rest of the van for carrying the kit.

I started back to work at my day job as a salesman two weeks after I got back on my drums and I was treated very well and I wasn't expected to overdo anything, but I am who I am and it wasn't long before I was working long days and evenings.

The first gig back after the initial two nights in Weymouth was playing at a wedding in The Old Mill at Batheaston and I wouldn't be kidding if I said I had to use all of my better driving skills to get into the parking area with the truck and trailer! The actual playing space and dance floor was tiny, but for all that we had a brilliant night.

My next gig was a little bit different because me, my bass player and Frank Aust, the leader of Hot Dog Jackson, went out as a band called Three of a Kind to Yeovil Labour Club which is a club my band The Sneakers play regularly. This was a one-off but we use Frank as a regular stand-in when required if either Billy or Chris is ill anytime.

The following Friday I had my pacemaker follow up by my heart surgeon, Ed Duncan, and that evening I played at a wedding with my band; the next day, I played at Wyke Regis Social Club in Weymouth.

The next Friday we played at Waterside Holiday Park Weymouth and Saturday Chesil Vista Holiday Park Weymouth, but we stayed in a caravan this time and we had the next weekend off. Our next gig was a skittles presentation at Haydon Que Club, a booking we do most years and the following Friday we played Waterside Holiday Park again.

The following week we played Weymouth Working Men's Club, another of our regular bookings, and on the Thursday of the following week we played at a new booking for us, it was in the Cumberland Hotel Bournemouth for a golden wedding. On the way down we were talking about what music should we play for a golden wedding but we needn't have worried because the first thing the couple said to us was did we play the Stones?! I was thinking more Glenn Miller! What a gig that turned out to be and the couple now come to our 60s weekends in Torquay. That weekend we played in The Dolphin, Ilchester, for our bass player's sister-in-law's 50th birthday.

Friends of mine got married the following Sunday and Mary and myself were invited as guests; the couple Julie and Clive, although they are karaoke singers, are regular followers of The Sneakers. My old mate Pat Mallon (sadly no longer with us) was there with Hayley and quite a lot of people I hadn't seen for years; the best man was Cliff Clarke whom I had encouraged to join a band and start singing seriously as he was a very good singer with a very strong voice: often he will get up to sing with us.

The following weekend was when I took Mary, Dave and Elaine to Torquay for what was supposed to be a Tinsel and Turkey weekend (it was a darts weekend unknown to us) and I was to put CDs, DVDs and letters of introduction advertising The Sneakers in all the hotels down the Belgrave

Road in Torquay. We enjoyed our weekend and then had to play a waiting game as to the result which, as shown earlier, was to our advantage.

The following Friday Mary had to go into hospital for an operation, one of many I am sorry to say, and she was in hospital the following day when I played at Yeovil Labour Club. A couple of weeks later I went to the Birmingham Indoor Arena to see The Who and they had Zak Starkey on drums: he was one of the best drummers I have had the privilege to watch live.

It was now December and Dave and Billy with myself played at our local football club Welton Rovers for the Midsomer Norton Community Trust Christmas Party, and the following night with the same line-up next door at the Midsomer Norton Social Club for a very well-known local character, Tony Day, for his building firm's annual Christmas party (he's a one-man band).

We always play the last Saturday before Christmas every year at Wyke Regis Working Men's Club and this year was no exception, and, as I had been ill and the band weren't sure I would ever get back to playing, Chris had taken a solo gig for New Year's Eve so I managed to get a local gig for me, Dave and Billy at the Midsomer Norton Social Club complete with bagpipes.

2013

2013 starts well with the first Saturday, we played at Cameley Lodge, a lovely country restaurant and special occasion venue, the only problem being that there is a noise limiter that is set so quiet that an acoustic guitar would set it off, but, us being us, we worked out how to bypass the system by running our power source from a 13-amp socket from the other side of the room, thereby not going into their system, but to make it look as if we were using the correct sockets we proceeded to put our stage lights through them! The following week we were back down Weymouth at the Working Men's Club on the harbour and that night after, a really good night. When we were on our way home from the club we only got about 50 yards and couldn't go any further: it turned out that someone had been stabbed in a nightclub at the end of the road. The outcome for us was that we had to drive through the pedestrian-only area to get back into the main street. Even though it was freezing cold, the girls walking about were wearing hardly any clothing and certainly no coats!

Back to the Social Club at Midsomer Norton on Friday, but Saturday was a night off. I was now working a four-day week at my day job which worked in well with my band commitments.

February starts off with a gig in Midsomer Norton Social Club; it almost feels as if we are resident but a gig is a gig and we are very popular at this club. The following day Mary and myself went to London for two days to celebrate my 65th birthday left over from January, and Mary had given me a boat trip down the Thames with a jazz band playing, but only my wife could organise a jazz band without a drummer, but they were very good and she was forgiven. We stayed at Islington and went by train into the centre of London; we even had a bit of snow and also did a fair bit of walking.

I then had the next weekend off and our next gig was Farrington Golf Club, and on the Saturday I played in Exeter with the band. Cliff Clarke sang as their drummer was unavailable; as it turned out it was not a bad night and if that wasn't unusual enough for me, the following Saturday I got to play the drums behind Elvis (local character Johny Morris) at a Masonic Ladies' Night at the Centurion Hotel. This was surreal, as I was a guest so had to put my kit up in the morning and in the evening the main act, an extremely talented female singer, had set her PA system up ready to start her show when the rest of Elvis's backing group turned up and started pulling wires out and shifting her kit all over the place, reducing her to tears as she had to reset the lot again!

When Johny Morris started he was like a man possessed and I actually think he believed he was ELVIS! The girl went on and did a good show. I personally was very embarrassed by the attitude of the other players and they didn't seem to understand what they had done to this girl. Needless to say, none of them play regularly in any bands.

The last week of March we went to Pontins at Brean for a four-day break but it was so cold. I am on warfarin and had to get my daughter to book us into a small hotel at Weston-super-Mare that had heating or we would have to go home, which wasn't really an option as my brother-in-law was decorating my house and had had the heating disconnected. We went home on Friday to find that our house had been flooded so it had turned out that it was a good decision to stay at Weston-super-Mare.

We played Easter Saturday at Yeovil Labour Club: usual good night and had to play a couple of encores. The following Saturday we played Wyke Regis Working Men's Club, and the following weekend was to be our first 60s weekend at the Rainbow Torquay. We really didn't know what to expect but we were introduced to Kate, the lady who had booked us, and to Marco, the actual owner of the hotel. On the first night I was called out of the dining room to be told that there was a group of unruly men on the stage where our equipment was set up. When I got in the ballroom I was confronted by a stag party most worse for wear through drink, so I went back to the dining room and got Marco. He sorted it out straight away by shutting the bar and sending them all out. We actually got some apologies over the weekend from some of the stag party.

The weekend went extremely well, so much so that we played there right up until September 2019, and there are many chapters to mention along the way. We didn't play the following week but the week after on the Friday we played at Coleford British Legion in the best hall by miles for acoustics, and the following day at Mardons Club Midsomer Norton.

The following Friday we played Dave Matthews' 50th birthday party and the Saturday at Haydon Que Club, a small but popular club and we always have a good night here. A couple of weeks later we played the Centurion Hotel as a three-piece band.

Paul Brimble

June.

We played at Yeovil Labour Club for the Crib Club presentation, a gig we did many times, and one of the players put us forward to the Langstone Cliff Hotel Dawlish where we have done many gigs to date. Found a new venue for us this Saturday: it was the Whisty Club Radstock. It was a private booking: great night, but we have not played there since; the acoustics were good as I recall.

July.

We played Frome Masonic Hall the first Saturday in July. It was a 80th birthday party and a very good night. I got to see a lot of old friends. We returned to Weymouth Working Men's Club for another good night: we actually filmed part of the show and it came out well. Back to Yeovil Labour Club the following week.

August.

Just Wyke Regis this month. August always a bit thin on the ground, most years the same; but hang on, we play on Friday 30th at Bristol Rovers Football Club for Gary Pinker, a well-known darts player in Bristol. He saw us playing at the Rainbow Torquay.

September.

We have been asked to play at Bruton in a really old building for a centenary of something or other, and there was a firework display and all sorts of other things going on; it was another good night. Friday 20th we got to play for Keith Brewer at our favourite venue, Coleford Legion, for his golden wedding. We also played for his wife's Line Dance troupe. It was a special night for me as Keith, locally known as Kipper, was instrumental in booking bands back in the 70s, including Spirelaine, one of my previous bands.

My Life with Music

October.

We played on Saturday which is unusual for us at Midsomer Norton Social Club as we normally play Fridays here and, the next Saturday was at Haydon Que Club for their annual skittles presentation. At the end of the month we played Bedminster Down Club with a so-called Robbie Williams tribute singer (I think false pretence would be the order of the day). We played well: it was a nice club with a massive stage.

November.

It seems that Kate from the Rainbow must have really enjoyed The Sneakers because for this 60s weekend in Torquay she invited all her friends and family to enjoy us and join her for her birthday: this was another brilliant weekend and we were rebooked for the following year. Our next booking was at the Centurion Hotel and that same weekend played Weymouth Working Men's Club, and then at the end of the month Yeovil Labour.

December.

The first Saturday in December we played Timsbury British Legion, and on the second Friday we played for the over-sixties Christmas party run by the local council, with the following night Tony Day's Christmas party and the following week at Wyke Regis Working Men's. On New Year's Eve I was able to put my ghosts to rest as we played Coleford British Legion, which was the same gig that I couldn't do because I had a stroke and had to get my son to play the gig for me. I had a standing ovation on the night and was very pleased when the night finished: it was a very good night and very emotional for me.

Paul Brimble

2014

My first gig was 18th of January at Timsbury British Legion with me, Dave and Billy. It was a very good night and we had our programme down to a fine art for the three of us. The following weekend we played Friday at a pre-63 Rock'n'Roll night, and the Saturday at a Burns Night, both gigs at Yeovil Labour Club. Billy played the bagpipes and addressed the haggis.

The following Saturday Billy, Chris and myself played at Frome Masonic Lodge for the Royal Somerset Lodge Ladies' Night. When we were setting up our kit, Alex the organiser gave me some leftover carpet to put in my van to cushion the sides and bulkhead.

I went to Frome Memorial Theatre the following Saturday to watch *That'll Be The Day*, a 50s and 60s musical show, and it was brilliant. When I went to my seat a lot of people spoke to me and asked me about the fact that there were two drum kits onstage, and was I going to get up and play? I just laughed it off! I soon found out why there were two drum kits up, as two brothers who were in the show played 'Dance With the Devil', a song made famous by Cozy Powell a few years earlier. The way they played it was absolutely MAGIC! And bear in mind all performers in the show sang and played various instruments, a show well worth going to.

Back to Weymouth Working Men's Club the next week as a three-piece, Billy, Chris and me, always a good night, and back to Coleford the week after, this time with all four of us. We finished February off with Billy, Dave and myself playing Midsomer Norton Social Club.

On the Saturday Dave and myself with our wives went for a meal at our bass player's from days gone by, Richard Doughty and his wife Jane who were living in Corsham, Wiltshire. (Richard played bass guitar for Spirelaine in the early days.) We saw one another occasionally and it was great to spend an evening with them.

The following Thursday I took a couple of my drum kits to St John's Junior School Midsomer Norton where two of my grandchildren went to school. Dave Stock brought a guitar and small amplifier to help me out in giving a lesson regarding drums. The children loved it and I also got the teachers involved. Dave played 'Apache' and 'Peaceful Easy Feeling' and, even though there were over 40 in the hall I let each child play either one or the other drums, or in some cases the complete kit, and towards the end of the session my daughter came in the hall and, to prove the drums were not only for the boys, proceeded to play the full kit. According to my granddaughter Georgia, she was now famous and all the kids wanted to be her friend!

The following Saturday I had to be assessed for my driving as I had a company car. The company insurance firm insisted on testing all the drivers. I passed but was picked up for driving too fast at times in built-up areas, but overall my driving was good.

Wyke Regis was our next booking and, as usual, was a good gig, with dancing from the first song until the last all four of us played. Billy flagged up that he wasn't available to play the whole of the following weekend, and we found out later that he had eloped to Gretna Green and got married to Jenny whom he had been with for years. We were surprised because she had proposed to him a couple of times and he said he would only marry her if she gave up smoking (but she hadn't).

The following Thursday I played at The Highwayman at Cannards Grave restaurant Shepton Mallet with Kevin and some others in a band we were thinking of forming called the Old Grey Whiskers Test. Kevin is well known for being the lead singer for The Mangledwurzels, a local Wurzels tribute band, but this venture was for him to get back to his first love, singing the blues. We did a couple of rehearsals and a couple of gigs; the other was Street Football Club playing on the back of a lorry, but we sort of fizzled out because we were too committed to our other musical interests.

We were then up to Easter Saturday and for quite a few years had a regular booking at Haydon Que Club with Billy myself and C.J., and as usual was a good night with plenty of people there to watch us. The next

Paul Brimble

Saturday we played Yeovil Labour Club with the full four-piece band on parade, and we had a very good reception and a full house but we always filled this club and they dance all night there. There is an elderly couple that jive with the man throwing his wife up in the air and doing moves that we wouldn't expect twenty-year-olds to do, let alone people in their seventies!

May Bank Holiday weekend we were asked to play the Friday night at the Langstone Cliff Hotel in Dawlish Warren where we were beginning to be part of the furniture. It was a gig we always looked forward to and we never knew what room we were going to play in, and this time it was the smaller room. We always seemed to get a better sound in the smaller room but the stage was a lot smaller and we were cramped a bit, but for all that we got over it and as always we were well fed with the same choice of food as the paying customers. For us it was a good gig for us to prepare for our 60s weekend the following week at the Rainbow International Hotel Torquay, and again this was a complete sell-out, with us picking up lots of accolades and a lot of new fans; also it was nice to see many of our new and existing friends.

On the following Friday we played at Yeovil Labour Club for a Crib Presentation where we actually got to meet the people who recommended us to the Langstone Cliff Hotel at Dawlish Warren, and they told us about the response they were given after The Sneakers played their first booking there. According to them, they could have walked on water at breakfast with all of the good compliments that they got about us.

On the Monday of the following week Mary and myself took my eldest son Charlie and my grandson Jaydon up to Liverpool to get the ferry over to the Isle of Man for the T.T. races which was a present for his 40th birthday. I had booked us in Pontins at Southport for a four-day break. (It was cheaper than driving home and back in my van.) I like Liverpool and we managed on the Friday to go to The Cavern before we met the ferry back from the Isle of Man. During my stay at Southport I was walking around the shops when I came across a shop selling the odd guitar and other musical items, so I went

My Life with Music

in and got talking to the man behind the counter. He told me he was in a famous Liverpool band in the 60s and on certain Sundays a lot of the old 60s players get together to jam and talk about the old times. Some of his stories were very interesting: I wish I had recorded them.

I suppose you could call our next gig boring but I don't do boring: it was Timsbury British Legion with our other three-piece combination of Dave, me and Billy: again a good night with a full crowd. I had a bit of a challenge the following week, as when you play in a band your diary gets filled long before family parties, weddings etc, and I had a booking on the Friday and a golden wedding party I had to be at as my wife Mary was a bridesmaid at the wedding, so this was to be a challenge but me, being me, got there. The Friday night booking was skittles presentation at Paulton Rovers Football Club, a long-standing booking that took place on the first Friday of June every year. I didn't get to bed before 2.00am but was on the road by 8.00am and the golden wedding party was in a hotel near Norwich about 180 miles away! I managed to get there with very little time to spare, and it was the first time I had time to really try out the Renault Trafic but at least I was in the RAC. All were surprised that I got there but I was determined that I would! The icing on the cake was that we were to stay the night at Sheringham, which is a lovely, small seaside town near Norwich, and on the Sunday we went to the beach where they had a street fayre with old-fashioned vehicles etc, and I drove back home later that day as I had to be back to work at my day job of selling windows on the Monday morning.

I must have been a glutton for punishment because the following Friday we played the Langstone Cliff Hotel Dawlish, and bearing in mind I don't get home until at least 3.30 in the morning to be set up and playing with the Old Grey Whiskers Test at Street Football Club in the afternoon was a task in itself, but then I had to be set up and playing at 8.00pm that night at Mardons Club Midsomer Norton but I managed all – not bad for someone who had written themself off three years earlier!

Paul Brimble

Wednesday the following week Mary and myself went to Taunton Cricket Ground to see Rod Stewart and what a show that was: the weather was perfect and I couldn't fault anything about the sound, the organising, everything was planned right down to the audience being bussed in. I would go again if the opportunity arose.

I went on holiday the following week with three days in Torquay and four days at one of our favourite caravan parks, Devon Cliffs, Exmouth, Devon.

July: didn't start until late for The Sneakers with only one booking and that was at Yeovil Labour Club, with only two bookings in August both in Weymouth: the first at Wyke Regis, one of the best venues we play in my view, and the following week Weymouth Working Men's Club, a much more spit and sawdust club.

C.J. does a few solo bookings in Weymouth and in September he was unavailable to play in the band for all but one Saturday. We played at Timsbury British Legion and that night they had a hog roast and a party (no particular reason that I can recall).

October: we played just two gigs!

November: we were back to Torquay for our sell-out three-nighter and then back to Yeovil Labour.

December starts with C.J. Billy and me playing Weymouth Workies, and the following week back to Midsomer Norton to play for the over-sixties Christmas party at Welton Rovers Football Club, then right next door at Midsomer Norton Social Club for Tony (dapper) Day's annual party. We were able to set up our kit straight after the first gig by getting in the club next door before they shut: they had cancelled the music for that night as most of their regular customers were to be at the over-sixties party where we were playing. Most years we play Wyke Regis Working Men's Club the last Saturday before Christmas, and this year was no exception, and then we finished the year with New Year's Eve at Timsbury British Legion where we did our usual New Year's Eve show with Dave Stock playing The Shadows

My Life with Music

to backing tracks and then The Sneakers. At 12.00 midnight Billy, our bass player, dressed in Highland dress, takes on his other persona as Billy the Piper with his bagpipes. The picture below shows Billy in full Highland dress, but with his bass guitar as opposed to his bagpipes.

For the first Friday of 2015 I took Mary to the pantomime in the Frome Memorial Theatre, a venue where I had played a few times myself in the orchestra pits supporting the Rotary Old Time Musicals with Kim and Dave, my fellow members of Spirelaine. The following day Dave, Billy and myself played at Midsomer Norton Social Club which, considering it was the first Saturday of the new year, was well attended and we had a good night.

The following Thursday we went to *Deal Or No Deal* in Bristol, a televised quiz show with Noel Edmonds, this was the second time we had been to the show. The first time was at Brislington, and this time it was the other side of Bristol in Whitchurch, and Mary actually appeared in a not very flattering position having to wear what I would call a Freddy the Parrot hat. But for all that, I have kept the recording of the programme at this time of writing. (Hopefully the Sagemcom recorder has a few years left in it!)

Later in the month we played St Annes Boardmills Club where we were getting to be one of their favourite bands according to Dave Plenty, who was the entertainment booker of the club.

When I was playing in Spirelaine we recorded two cassette albums at Potterne with Pete Lamb, and now he runs a jam session in The Bear at Devizes, so Dave Stock and myself went on the following Thursday where Pete greeted us like long-lost brothers; we both ended up playing. I went to a couple more jam sessions at Devizes, but because of the distance decided it was too far away.

My mates were all going to a Rock'n'Roll weekend at Sand Bay near Weston-super-Mare, so Dave Stock and myself and our wives decided to go with them, albeit we had to play ourselves on the Saturday night as The Sneakers had a gig in Yeovil. I like a certain amount of Rock'n'Roll but I

Paul Brimble

think we ended up with the best deal as the music that was being played at Sand Bay was pure rock and roll. It was so boring that all of us ended up in the karaoke bar on the Sunday night, and Dave sang a few songs which went down very well. I would say most of the audience felt the same as us, as the karaoke bar was filled to capacity!

We were to play the Langstone Cliff Hotel for the Friday night of their Valentine weekend, a gig we get every year now, and on the Saturday Wyke Regis Working Men's Club at Weymouth which falls on the same weekend year on year, always a good night.

Melksham has a very good club: it is called Spencers and they have once a month 60s or Rock'n'Roll bands and it is a great atmosphere. We have up to this time played it three times but when you see the bands available to play this I think we have done quite well!

Even though Spencers was a good gig for us and our following, the next Saturday we played St Annes Boardmills Club, still one of our favourite clubs to play where they dance the first song through to the last and make you feel great.

Mary and myself like to go away for our wedding anniversary to Devon Cliffs in Exmouth only for three or four days, but we have struck up a friendship with a lovely family that run a popular cafe in Exmouth and whenever we turn up we are greeted like part of their family, which is really nice. We came home on the Friday and then we drove into Bath to the Bath Spa Hotel to have an afternoon tea (very posh!). It was a prize I won in a raffle: to say we felt like gypsies was an understatement! But it was a nice finish to a week's holiday.

The band played at Dawlish Easter Saturday and this time we performed in the large room at the Langstone Cliff Hotel, and to be quite honest I prefer playing in the smaller room, even though we are a bit cramped on the stage: this room seems a bit more intimate, whereas the large room feels cold and the sound seems to drop off about two-thirds into the room. It was a reasonable night and we received quite a lot of good accolades.

At the end of April The Sneakers played at the Fry Club Keynsham and all songs had to be pre-1963: I did a list of songs to suit. With all four of us playing it meant we had three singers so it made my job a bit easier as Dave did most of the ballads, and C.J. and Billy the more upbeat songs; also, because we had rhythm and lead guitarists, we were able to do some early Shadows numbers like 'Apache', 'Theme For Young Lovers' and 'Sleepwalk'. The Fry Club like The Sneakers because of the mix of songs that they play.

At the beginning of May we played Hythe and District Social Club near Southampton. This is a club that heard about us on a coach trip to Weymouth where they saw C.J. playing a solo gig and he told Tony their entertainments manager about The Sneakers. He booked us and up until now has given us two bookings every year which suits me owing to the distance we have to travel, but on the plus side music has to finish at 11.00pm which means we get home at a reasonable time about 2.00am, especially as Billy and myself were setting up for our next gig at 12.00 noon which was a local one at the Haydon Que Club, Radstock, the town where Billy lives, and this is always a good gig but we play it as a three-piece without Dave.

Our 60s weekend at Torquay is next and as usual is good. We make a lot of new friends and I decided to stay for the rest of the week until the Friday, staying on a caravan park in Torquay. I couldn't stay any longer as I had a booking on the Saturday at Timsbury British Legion with our other three-piece line-up, Dave, Billy and me. We are always popular over at that club and a lot of our friends who had been to Torquay also came and were raving about the 60s weekend.

The skittles presentation which we had played for more than ten years was to be our last one because of lack of interest, and to be quite honest it really had run its course. The venue was Paulton Rovers Football Club, but for it to be a good night you needed a couple of hundred in the room to fill it;

there were about 130 at the start, but when the presentation was over there can't have been 50 left in the room. All the younger people went to either Bath or Bristol clubbing it, and the ones left were mostly older men. They enjoyed listening to the music but the organisers decided it wasn't worth the effort that they had put in and pulled the plug on it. We still do the summer league presentation but that is on a much smaller scale and in another venue.

Mary bought me for Father's Day tickets for us both to go to the Bristol Hippodrome the following Thursday to see the Jersey Boys and I thoroughly enjoyed it. I had also the year before seen the 'Let's Hang On' show in Frome and I thought that show had the edge. It could have been the sound in the smaller theatre; I couldn't put my finger on it but that was the show I enjoyed most out of the two.

Dave Burfoot, who was my vocalist in Spirelaine, had a brother Alan and I hadn't seen him for years until Dave's funeral. We got talking about music and the old days and Alan told me he helped with the entertainments at a British Legion Club in Bristol and asked if I would like to play there. Obviously I was interested and we agreed terms, and The Sneakers were invited to play at Bishopsworth British Legion and soon became a part of the furniture. The first booking we did, Billy, Dave and myself set the kit up at midday and Alan was there to greet us. He hyped us up so much to the others at the club that we daren't let him down but, like all the other clubs, we play there regularly now. We played Yeovil Labour the following week and the week after was Glastonbury; no, we didn't get to play it, but I was asked to put a band together to cover for a band that had been asked to play Glastonbury last-minute and could I cover their booking in Clevedon. Dave and C.J. were unavailable but I was able to get Frank Aust from Hot Dog Jackson, a very talented guitarist whom I had used before and still do now on the odd occasion, and we did the gig, it was a family party and according to Ian Hobbs, the singer from The Honky-Tonks which was the band we covered for, we did them proud and all the guests really enjoyed our music.

My Life with Music

We had no bookings for a couple of weeks so I booked a holiday with *The Sun* newspaper; actually it was two holidays back to back at Hendra, one of the biggest caravan parks in Newquay, Cornwall. The weather was lovely but the caravan that we were booked into had a horrible smell to it: I think someone had been sick in it and the caravan had not been cleaned up properly. We complained and the staff immediately had the van completely steam-cleaned and we were able to sleep in it that night thinking that it was sorted, but the following day we went out all day and when we came back so had the smell! It was really overpowering. I can put up with some things but not that, so I complained at the office again and this time we were moved into one of their brand new, extra-wide caravans with every conceivable extra you could think of in it and proceeded to have one of the best holidays in Cornwall that we have ever had.

Our next booking was for Dave, Billy and myself to play at Midsomer Norton Social Club, and this was a normal club night with a decent attendance. Mary has a long-standing problem which needs periodic pain injections which are done at the Pain Clinic in the RUH Bath. So on the Thursday afternoon I drove her in and waited for a phone call to say she was ready as I went about my day job. On the Saturday, Dave, Billy and myself played Timsbury British Legion, another regular gig, and as always there was a large audience.

August is always a slow month for us as C.J. has his solo commitments playing in hotels in Weymouth, but this year we had two: the first was Yeovil Labour Club, always popular for us, and the other one was at Wyke Regis where, as the weather was good, we went earlier in the morning and called in for a cup of tea with Mike Weeks who, with his wife before she died, used to follow the band wherever they could and even booked us to play at their golden wedding. In September Mary and myself had a week's holiday in the Isle of Wight and thoroughly enjoyed it, so much we decided we would go again. The Sneakers played the Langstone Cliff Hotel for one of their loyalty weekends, and we were well received as usual.

October was busy we played Midsomer Norton two weeks on the trot: one a club night, the other a skittles presentation, and the following week Haydon Que for another skittles presentation. The weekend after we did some distance bookings: on the Friday Hythe and District near Southampton (they love us there) and on the Saturday the Langstone Cliff Hotel at Dawlish Warren, but the following week I had a break as I had to be a guest at my sister Delphine's golden wedding (her husband Roger was unable to attend as he was ill in hospital). I was given plenty of notice so that I wouldn't take a booking on that particular day. I was almost commanded that I should be there so imagine the ribbing I gave her when her own husband couldn't make it. I must admit I had said all along that Roger wouldn't be there, but at least he had a good excuse!

My brother Barry and Delphine hadn't spoken to each other for as many years as I could remember, and I often told each of them that they needed their heads bashing together, and in years to come they would regret falling out. Delphine also fell out with my mother and they didn't speak for the last seventeen years of my mum's life.

Two weeks later we had one of our 60s weekends in the Rainbow Torquay and it was billed as a Tinsel and Turkey 60s weekend and Billy played the bagpipes on the Sunday night: the audience were amazed as they had never witnessed anything like this before. The owner Marco was over the moon and had posters and advertising done, including a discount for booking for our May weekend if they booked before leaving to go home.

Back then on our usual local gig at Timsbury the following Saturday, and there were a lot of people there that had been to Torquay with us and were raving about how they had enjoyed the weekend, and also the fact we played three nights without repeating a song!

The Sneakers played a private gig at Farrington Golf Club the following Saturday, not one of the easiest places to get into and set up: not only do we

My Life with Music

have to go upstairs, but then we also have to open up a false fireplace to put our cases etc away and we are left with a very small area to set up and there is no stage. Despite all that we ended up having a good night.

Both Billy and C.J. were unable to play the following week so I didn't take any bookings, but then we were into the Christmas season. Friday night we played for the over-sixties Christmas party which is arranged by the local council and there are two venues to choose from for the council to hold this function. Welton Rovers Football Club is our preference as opposed to the town hall, but this year we drew the short straw and it was the town hall.

There are a couple more disadvantages for playing the town hall. Firstly, the hall is used by various organisations and we have to set up early in the morning, not a big problem except it doesn't open early enough for us to get in and set up before the first organisation needs the room. Lucky for us one of the staff did us a favour by coming in an hour early so we were able to set up. The next problem is getting in at night, and unless you are used to having functions often with live music, allowing the band time to be ready before the public arrive.

The council bus them in and supply the food and drink and one minute there is no one there, and then there is a coachload and they are all starving and we have trouble trying to sound-check and balance the volume as they expect you to start 'just like that!' but we are used to it and take it in our stride.

The next night we played at Midsomer Norton Social Club for Tony Day's Christmas party, both nights as a three-piece, Dave, Billy and myself. As it is only a week before Christmas we played on the Friday at Dawlish for one of these Christmas parties where quite a few companies choose to take their staff to a hotel for Christmas parties with live band, disco and Christmas menu. The disco we played with was very arrogant and Billy took a dislike to him which proved to be right, as he made it very difficult for us to start our second set after him. On the Saturday we played Wyke Regis Working Men's Club and we thoroughly enjoyed it, as did the crowd. The following Tuesday I went to Bath Racecourse for my Christmas meal and party with Techniglaze, the company I worked for.

This New Year we played a three-nighter at the Rainbow Hotel Torquay. I really needed a break when we got home, on reflection the three nights are too much! We look on it as a small holiday, but as soon as I got home I had to think about taking the decorations down and getting ready to go back to work to start another year.

2016

The first gig this year was St Annes Boardmills Club in Bristol. This club is without doubt the best run club that we play. Dave Plenty, the entertainments manager, has put this club on the map. He books entertainment every Friday, Saturday and Sunday, and promotes them all the time. The club is just like it used to be in the, dare I say it, 'OLDEN DAYS' when the clubs were full you had a job to park your car in the car park and then they danced from the first song until the last: those were the days. Well, this is as near as it gets and long may it last!

We then played for our regular Burns Night at Yeovil Labour Club with Billy toasting the haggis and playing the bagpipes, and then back local the week after to Timsbury British Legion.

A new venue to us was Spencer Social Club Melksham. It is primarily a Rock'n'Roll club but the organisers had seen us in Torquay and decided 60s Rock'n'Roll was alright for them and we went down very well. There was also a Rock'n'Roll disco whom we got on with very well and have worked with numerous times since.

For some reason we seem to play Dawlish and Weymouth most Valentine weekends and this was no exception. My wife doesn't really like me doing these long distances at my age as I do all the driving, but as I tell her, this is how the bookings fall and I really have no choice in the matter.

The following weekend we were local, with the weekend after playing

My Life with Music

at the Red Post Peasedown St John for the most unpopular landlord in the West Country he is so arrogant and charges extortionate prices for drinks. He booked us and then told us on the night that all his regulars had gone to Butlins this particular weekend and proceeded to tell us we were the most expensive band that he books. Well, as you can imagine, the place was almost empty and the cheeky git said to me, 'I thought you were popular,' so I told him in no uncertain terms that our job wasn't to bring people in but to entertain the people that did so that they didn't leave, and no one did leave! We have decided not to play there again.

I took a booking for the daughter of a woman who had booked us for a charity gig a few years previously thinking it was another gig for charity. Well, about six weeks before we were to play the gig I decided to contact the mother and try to advertise it on Facebook, but unknown to me the gig was a surprise birthday present from her family and obviously she knew nothing about it. Her daughter rang me to tell me what I had done, but she had the peace of mind to tell her mother that we were playing this particular night in Frome Town Football Club and that she had managed to get tickets for her and her father to come, so I was let off the hook! I have seen her a few times since and we always have a laugh about it now. It was a busy weekend: we played Mardons Club on the Saturday, but their new premises are not as good as their old club as far as we are concerned.

Bishopsworth British Legion. This was the last time I was to see Alan Burfoot before he died. He was struggling a bit on the night but we met up with him in the morning when we set up. As usual, another good night in Bristol. Billy, C.J. and myself finished March off in Haydon Que Club where a lot of our mates turned up.

A couple of weeks later I had to have a pacemaker check and, although I had been having them once a year since I had it fitted, it was now showing up that it only had a battery life of less than two years, so I had to have a check at three-month intervals; I had the weekend off that week. The week after,

Paul Brimble

Dave, Billy and myself played our usual gig at Timsbury British Legion, and the following Friday the full band played at Dawlish with no gigs on the Saturday, but on the Sunday we played in the new Somerdale Pavilion in Keynsham. This was the building that replaced the Fry Club after it was demolished for a new housing estate to be built. The old Fry Club was a difficult building to set up at. It was upstairs and when Spirelaine played there we had problems going up the steel staircase that was on the outside of the building. Whoever made the staircase had the long end of the bolts on the inside of the framework, and they caught on our clothes as we tried to carry the kit in, and with a Hammond organ, a Yamaha electric piano, Logan Strings and a Sharma rotary cabinet besides a PA system and full drum kit, we found it extremely hard to get in and God help us when it rained! I even kept putting up the prices hoping they would stop booking us, but we were so popular they didn't. The Somerdale Pavilion on the first occasion proved a problem getting in, but afterwards we found a way in through the front entrance and were able to use the lift. We organised ourselves to each doing our individual bits get it off to a fine art. The gig was a wedding anniversary for friends of ours, Stuart and Margaret Tibbs. They followed The Sneakers all over the place, including many of our weekends in Torquay. The gig went well and we were well pleased with the overall sound, as we had been told that other bands didn't like the sound that they got in the new club. Dave Bateman, the promoter for Rock'n'Roll nights in the Somerdale Pavilion, was a guest: he liked what he heard and has booked us on numerous occasions since.

Off to Hythe next and then to Torquay for yet another sell-out 60s weekend. I stayed for the rest of the week at Torquay which was getting to be a habit for our May weekends. Midsomer Norton Social Club was to be our next booking for just three of us, and on the Saturday with all four of us we were off to Dawlish again. This time we set our kit up and went for a walk down to the beach as the weather was beautiful.

My Life with Music

The gig we really look forward to, St Annes Boardmills, was the week after, and then off to Yeovil, Timsbury, Midsomer Norton, Melksham and Wyke Regis, and then a month off. At the end of September Mary and myself with friends of ours, Sue and Nick Wylle, went to Ilfracombe for a 60s weekend with loads of 60s bands there: Union Gap, Vanity Fair and Herman's Hermits, to name a few. There was a band on midday on the Sunday that were brilliant and I struck up a friendship with the drummer Keith Slater who also was the vocalist. They were a very tasty band and I was very impressed. Their rendition of 'Flingel Bunt' was the best I have ever heard from any band!

October we were out quite a bit – Haydon Que, Bishopsworth, Hythe and St Annes – and then into November, Mardons, Torquay, Midsomer Norton and Timsbury, only for me to interrupt proceedings having to go to London for the British Heart Foundation to have a photo shoot and interview for their *Heart Matters* magazine and then to finish 2016 at Yeovil, a couple in Midsomer Norton, then Wyke Regis and New Year's Eve.

Heart matters

Timsbury, and what a night that was: it was the first time that we had used the full four-piece band in this club as the stage is very small, but we managed with two on the stage and two on the floor, making sure that the fire door was still accessible to get out. We proceeded to have an excellent night that was, according to many, the best New Year's Eve that the club had ever had.

My Life with Music

2017

I should have left my kit up at Timsbury Legion as Dave, Billy and myself played there on the first Saturday of the new year which also was my 69th birthday. There was no bookings then for a couple of weeks so I managed to book a so-called 60s break at Pontins Sand Bay but met with disappointment as it was a load of solo singers with backing tracks and not bands which was what I was expecting and there were many guests that felt the same, but we got no apologies from Pontins.

It was now our second visit to Somerdale Pavilion and a lot of our friends as well as the usual rock'n'rollers were there, and we were given a great reception and told we would be invited back. Saturday night we played at Yeovil Labour Club for the annual Burns Night with Billy playing the bagpipes and toasting the haggis. We then did our regular bookings at Midsomer Norton Social Club, Wyke Regis, Langstone Cliff St Annes, Welton Rovers Football Club and Timsbury Legion, and then we played Dundry British Legion. We were recommended by someone that had seen us playing at Torquay the previous year, he wanted us to play two gigs for him, but we were only available for one.

We played Hythe and District Social Club the following Friday and didn't play for the next three weeks as two of the band were unavailable; the first booking back was Bishopsworth British Legion and Alan Burfoot couldn't make it as he was struggling with his health. We did miss him as he always made us feel very welcome. We were then up to Easter Saturday and off to Dawlish where we played in the larger room. The next Saturday Billy, C.J. and I played for a 70th birthday party at Standerwick Market Hall. The Sneakers had played here only once before but Spirelaine loads of times, mostly for Rotary functions but also a few private parties. This birthday party was for Dave Sergent, someone that I knew from my schooldays, and he eventually met up with one of Mary's friends, Anne Monger, from Buckland Dinham, the village she grew up in, and many years later they got married. They must have enjoyed the band as they turned up with another couple to one of our Torquay weekends two weeks later!

We were then back on our regular gigs – Midsomer Norton Social Club, Haydon Que, Timsbury British Legion, St Annes Boardmills, Mardons – and surprise, surprise I had relented and taken a gig at the Red Post (this gig was certainly better than the previous one) and I took another one for later in the year. Whitchurch British Legion was a new venue for us with the person in charge of entertainment having seen us in another club she was associated with wanting us there, but she could only afford the three-piece: Billy, C.J. and myself. It was a lovely club, large and well laid out, and we went down very well to the not too big audience. I had a wedding to go to the following weekend in Bognor Regis and we had a long weekend away in a caravan, and when we got back I was due another pacemaker check that week to be told I was to have another fitted in September.

August is always flat for us booking-wise but we had one three-piece with Dave, Billy and me in Timsbury Legion and the full band at Wyke Regis.

6th September I went to the RUH in Bath to be fitted with my second pacemaker. When I had my first I was told it should last about fifteen years; well. mine lasted five and I was told it was because of my drumming, but also it was good for me to carry on, and they don't mind how many times I have to have a replacement. I didn't have any bookings for the whole of September to allow for the wound to heal.

The first booking back was a skittles presentation at Haydon Que Club, and the week after we supported Tank Sherman at Bishopsworth British Legion. He is a brilliant comedian and a nice person. We worked with him once before and I have seen him a couple of times, besides always managing to have a chat with him.

Poster for Tank Sherman supported by The Sneakers

We played Hythe the week after, always a good night, but it's an 11.00pm finish so, even though it's a long journey, I am normally in bed before three in the morning. Then our next booking was a local one in Midsomer Norton and the following night we played a 60s show in Trowbridge with Russ Matthews, a very good solo artist, also featuring Dave playing The Shadows, and The Sneakers playing two sets; we even had a coachload of our supporters from Midsomer Norton – most were at the previous night's booking! Russ Matthews was very impressed with us and the show was a virtual sell-out.

The next two months were very busy for us as we had gigs every weekend up until Christmas: Dawlish, Bristol, Torquay, Peasedown, Midsomer Norton and Weymouth included. New Year's Eve we played at Spencer Social Club Melksham, again starting the evening with Dave Stock playing The Shadows, and The Sneakers playing three sets, and Billy piping in at midnight, all of this ably assisted by Roger the DJ.

This was to be a sad night for the band as this was Dave's last night: he had decided to retire, and after all, he was almost 80! It was sad for me because Dave had been with me for about 45 years with Spirelaine, The Sultans and The Sneakers, but as with all New Year's Eve gigs it was a brammer of a gig!

The first gig in 2018 was for my 70th birthday party which meant, even though Dave had retired, he came out of retirement to play at my party. I was privileged to have my son Shane and my daughter both at different intervals play the drums onstage with my band. During the evening I presented Dave with a framed picture of the band and I made a speech thanking him for his many years of being in bands with me. To my embarrassment my wife did a *This Is Your Life* on me and had everybody in stitches about some of the things that I had done in my past. Instead of presents I had a raffle and a charity collection for the British Heart Foundation which made over £600 and I presented the cheque to the local branch.

Me presenting a cheque to the British Heart Foundation

My Life with Music

When I was seventeen four of us had our photograph taken outside of the photographer's studio in Radstock Road, Midsomer Norton, and we have stayed friends ever since. We decided my 70th birthday party would be a good place to have one taken again 50-odd years later.

Tony Higgins, Ray Rogers, Roger Jones, Paul Brimble

Left to right: Tony Higgins, Ray Rogers, Roger Jones and Paul Brimble

50 years later. Left to right: Roger Jones, Paul Brimble, Ray Rogers and Tony Higgins

Paul Brimble

January is normally slow for bookings but this year we had my 70th, a 60th, a Rock'n'Roll night, a golden wedding and a couple of club bookings: the month was looking good. February didn't start quite so well as the first booking, a ladies' night at Frome Masonic, was cancelled due to lack of interest but we did manage to play three more gigs that did take place, two in Bristol and a Valentine's dance in Dawlish.

The first weekend in March Mary, myself and some friends were going down to the Riviera Hotel at Torquay for two nights as a break but it snowed quite heavily and it got cancelled. The following week we played Timsbury British Legion for Joan Allen, the lady who took the money on the door: it was her 90th birthday party and luckily the snow had gone. On the following Friday there were warnings about the beast from the east (snow) coming back and we had to drive to Hythe near Southampton to play. I picked Billy up as usual and all seemed well. Just as we got to Salisbury, Billy said he felt as if he was going down with a cold. We played the booking and by the time I dropped him home about 3.00 in the morning he was burning up! We were due to play a charity gig the following day but the warnings of very heavy snow were threatening whether it should be cancelled.

I contacted the organiser and was hoping it would get cancelled as Billy was ill and not really able to sing, and also I didn't want to be responsible if Chris couldn't get home to Weymouth. In the end Ruth Travis, the organiser, made the decision to cancel (I had told her she had until 5.00pm to cancel, as once Chris left Weymouth we would expect to be paid). We don't charge cancellation fees, neither do we take deposits, so that it would cost her nothing to cancel. Being a charity we didn't want them to incur costs, but believe it or not, Frome Town Football Club charged full cost for the room and it was right to cancel as we had over a foot of snow that night!

Mary and myself had our own celebration the next week: it was our ruby wedding and we went away with our family to Poole for the weekend, all except Shane, Kate Woody and Ziggy who came down on the Sunday and we all went out for a celebration meal. The band finished the week off at Wyke Regis Working Men's Club.

April was a lean month bookings-wise as we played two bookings the first weekend and one the last weekend with nothing in between. The first Saturday in May was to be a tricky one: we were to play at a 60th birthday in a pub for Billy's brother-in-law Stan. We had played this pub twice before and we weren't very happy that it was such a small room with hardly any space for us to put up our kit. When I got there Chris was leaving the pub with a cob on, saying no way was he going to be able to set up his kit in the room allocated and that me and Billy were to play the gig as a duo!

It turned out that Billy had had a row with the landlady and if it wasn't for the fact that Stan was his brother-in-law she could go take a run, but we had to make the best of a bad job. I didn't think it would be possible to get away with what was being proposed, but had a few years previously seen Billy play at a function with another drummer (it was during the time that I was getting over my stroke), a friend of mine, Brian Smalley, and they got away with it so I decided that was what we had to do. Believe it or not, we had a brilliant night and it was playing stuff that mostly I had never done before! The party went well and Stan was over the moon that we were able to play all night, so much so that he paid us the full price and I gave Chris his cut as it certainly wasn't his fault that we didn't have enough room for all of us to be able to play.

We were back to Torquay the following Friday, Saturday and Sunday, another brilliant weekend at the Riviera Hotel and this led onto a run of our favourite clubs, St Annes and Bishopsworth. We then did a golden wedding party in a club that we had never been to before, a place called Blackfield not far from Hythe. This was on the Friday; we had the Saturday off and played on the Sunday for a wedding at North Wootton near Wells. This weekend must have been one of the hottest weekends of the year. Luckily for us, we were able to play outside on a sheltered raised patio. It turned out that the bride was a hairdresser at the salon where Billy, our bass player, has his hair cut!

Back to the normal club bookings the following week and then we played at my cousin's 60th birthday and it was held at St Annes Boardmills Club, Bristol. Mary had an operation at the R.U.H. that day and I was able to get to see her after her operation on the way to the gig, despite her telling me not to. We played well, the party was good, and I got to see relatives I hadn't seen for years and even some I didn't even know. The downside of the night was that I had trouble starting the van at the end of the evening and needed a push to get it going.

We were at Hythe the following Friday and were given many good accolades regarding the golden wedding party that we had played at a month before.

Back to Timsbury Legion for a usual Saturday club night and then we had a booking in a naturist club in the middle of a forest near Ringwood. I knew the organiser as we had played for him before for an organisation called Leroc, a sort of salsa dancing club around Yeovil and Bridgwater, and we had also played for them at Weymouth.

The weather wasn't very good: in fact we had rain, hail and thunder and lightning, which in a way saved a bit of embarrassment because the guests kept their clothes on, or at least until the end, and then one of the women who had been virtually flashing all night stripped completely naked. Well, you can imagine what we were faced with if I said that she had five children and a C-section scar, and was grossly overweight (and I am being very polite): not a very good view and, not to be outdone, one of the men stripped off to dance with her; luckily for us it was the very end of the evening. When we were packing down the woman didn't bother to dress and was talking to us as if it was quite normal! None of us were impressed.

The band had all but the last weekend in August off with just our usual gig in Wyke Regis. We had a couple in September, one with Micky John Bull, a famous West Country comedian/singer, and he was good. We got on very well and worked the audience well between us. We were then back to each weekend in October.

November we were back to the Riviera Hotel Torquay for our usual 60s sell-out weekend and then back to normal club bookings. December we did a lot of mileage: we played Dawlish, Bristol, Wyke Regis and Torquay to end 2018.

2019 started on the second Saturday of the year at Timsbury British Legion and I got a phone call 9.00am from my lead guitarist Chris to say he could play but had a bad chest and also a very bad throat, so bad he wouldn't be able to sing. I managed to get Frank Aust to dep for us at very late notice: it was right for me to rest Chris as we had two bookings the following weekend and I needed to make sure we were able to play both.

Billy had bought an expensive PA speaker system and was having problems with setting up the mixer. He had bought the mixer from Chris and relied on him to get the right balance, so on the night we had an absolute disaster with the vocal sound, i.e. too loud (poor old Frank was completely drowned out) and Billy brought the volume of his bass guitar with it!

During our break I was absolutely savaged about it, but as I was on the stage and the audience were clapping I didn't realise we had a problem. I had words with Billy and we did the best we could to get the sound right, but the damage had been done so then it was down to damage limitation. Our usual followers gave us the benefit of doubt and most said it was a good night in the end, but I was put through the wringer the following week down at the local cafe. It cost the band a cancellation as we had been booked for a party later in the year, and the customers decided to come and see us that night and to show us off to some friends that they had brought with them, but they ended up walking out and eventually cancelling the band.

The Sneakers were back to full strength the following Friday for a Rock'n'Roll night in Somerdale Rock'n'Roll club Keynsham where we played all songs pre-1963. It's a gig we really like as the stage is big, the room is welcoming, the audience are great, we have a sympathetic DJ, and the venue has a lift to get our kit in, not to forget Dave Bateman the man that books us – he is a gentleman. At the end of the night when we were packing up I found a pair of PA speaker stands left on the loading area in front of the venue and, as everybody had gone, I put them in my van for safety.

The following morning I rang the DJ and, sure enough, they were his and I arranged with him that as I was going to set up that lunchtime in St Annes Boardmills Club, and as he lived in Bristol I would leave them there for him to pick up later on. He got to the club before we left and was very grateful for my honesty and would put our name around the places he works.

St Annes is one of our favourite clubs and this particular night Dave Plenty, the entertainments manager, recorded four songs for their Facebook page and we milked this as best we could for our benefit. We tackle some songs that other bands wouldn't dream of and the one that really shows us off is 'Nights in White Satin', a Moody Blues song. Billy really does the song justice, but as a band The Sneakers are able to call on approximately nine hours of songs without repeating any, and with all the years we have been together have never had what could be called a proper rehearsal (we might run through the odd song when we are set up at Torquay) but we will tackle anything if asked!

After the previous week we were good and back on song with our next gig to be a Burns Night at Yeovil. It was a good night: we saw a lot of our old friends and it was reasonably packed, especially as it was a Friday and we usually play Saturdays. We have three more bookings there this year and all said they were looking forward to seeing us.

A local gig at Midsomer Norton followed the next week and then a bit of travelling for us as it was Valentine's weekend: the Friday was at the Langstone Cliff Hotel Dawlish and Saturday Wyke Regis where it was absolutely packed. They danced all night, always a good crowd with lots of good comments.

Timsbury British Legion, we had to get this gig right after the fiasco in

My Life with Music

January and boy, did we!? As Simon Cowell would say we hit the ball out of the park! It was a great night and we got our reputation back; not only that but we played the following Thursday afternoon for the Midsomer Norton Community Afternoon Club for their 6th birthday party. It was their best attended function in all the six years by the local community and The Sneakers were put down as the main reason and we certainly got some accolades.

I have been playing local jam sessions in Frome and Midsomer Norton and have made friends with a lot of fellow musicians, and I have met up with some old friends and made some new ones: Brian Talbot, whom I had the pleasure of playing drums with way back in the 70s, and Taffy Whitcombe, a drummer who used to share the stool with me at jam sessions at Maiden Bradley and Warminster in the 90s, and I have got friendly with Roger Davenport, a really talented guitarist, and his wife Annie, a brilliant tenor sax player, and I have been rehearsing a bit with them both and also a bass player.

Mary and myself went to the Riviera Hotel in Torquay to celebrate our friends' golden wedding where we had to watch entertainment (singers with backing tracks), not live bands, but it was with good company and we enjoyed the break.

I did my first Heart Foundation talk to a ladies' group at Paulton and was told I did quite well! One lady gave me her bingo money as a donation.

Our next booking was to Hythe near Southampton, and this was an extremely good night for us: the club was packed and we kept them right up to the end of the evening. We then played our regular Easter Saturday gig at Haydon Que Club and the club was packed. We had another brilliant night. Easter Sunday, Mary and myself went to a wedding: the weather was really hot unusually as it was still only April.

The following Friday we were back to Torquay playing our three-night weekender. Friday night was good but I made a decision which I now regret which was to play two sets and then retire to the balcony and do an impromptu acoustic session (but it didn't work). We were accused of short-changing our followers by finishing early. That night I didn't sleep a wink worrying what everybody felt about us. The following night we more than made up for it, but after we finished there was a spot of trouble with one of our following getting up on the stage after we had finished and getting shouted at by Chris, and a few took exception, including my wife, and I am afraid we had words about it. As far as I am concerned, Chris was right when you think about the cost of our equipment on the stage and the fact that the person on the stage had no chance of paying for any damage if any was done.

Sunday was alright but, by then, I had made my mind up that enough was enough regarding running a band and had made my mind up that I was going to leave The Sneakers at the end of the year. On Friday we played Midsomer Norton Social Club and I told Billy of my intention to leave the band: he was quite understanding and he said that The Sneakers was the longest he had ever been in one band and knew that it would come to an end sometime. He also said that he wanted to move back to Scotland in the near future, and now the timing might be right to give it some consideration. I hadn't mentioned it to Chris yet and I wanted to pick my moment.

The following Saturday we played Whitchurch British Legion and I decided I would talk to him there. I told him that I had made my mind up to leave the band, and also what Billy had said about Scotland I also said about his failing health and my concerns there, and he mentioned that he was considering buying a camper van and doing some travelling. We all decided we would finish at the end of the year and, as we didn't want to play our last night at Babbacombe, that I should cancel and if possible get a booking in its place where we would be in front of our faithful followers.

Monday night was jam night at The White Hart, Midsomer Norton, and I and one other drummer were in attendance on the night of which I played the lion's share of the songs. I actually finished at 12.20 in the morning.

Tuesday evening Mary and myself were treated by another couple to their wedding anniversary evening watching Marty Wilde on his 80th birthday tour at the Octagon Yeovil and as a thankyou I paid for a meal for us all to celebrate.

On Wednesday morning I had a phone call from Roger Davenport to ask if I could help him out on a rehearsal with a band he was putting together as the drummer they were using was going on a tour with Phil Collins for three weeks, so I helped out.

This Friday we played at Coleford British Legion for a golden wedding party. The hall is one of the best halls for sound that we ever get the chance to play in. We had a few problems with the electric but found out later we were using the wrong sockets as they had been condemned because of a fire, but overall we had a great sound and a good night.

Saturday morning I got a phone call to say that Chris's father-in-law Derek had died. It was expected but as we had a booking at Yeovil Labour Club could I get someone else to take Chris's place that night? I tried but our usual stand-in Frank was out playing with another band. I decided to cancel. I had cancelled gigs before but not on the day, this was the first one I had ever cancelled on the day: and bearing in mind I have run bands since 1973 it's not a bad legacy!

The fact that I had to cancel on the day of the gig really hurt me and, even though the club concerned were very understanding, I was more intent on finishing at the end of the year and, having made up my mind, wanted to tell certain people and I intimated to a few but said that it was a possibility.

Our next booking was at Haydon Que Club for a 70th birthday party: it was for one of our loyal followers, Mike Beacham. Sadly, there weren't too many there but we had a very good sound that night and everyone there really enjoyed themselves. The following night I went to two clubs on the same night as I didn't have a gig. Mary wanted to go to Timsbury British Legion where she goes most Saturdays if she doesn't go with me and the band, and good friends of mine The Two of Clubs were playing at Westhill Club. Mark and Dave are two of the nicest people I know in our business: they have the attitude and ability to entertain any audience whatever age!

Paul Brimble

I stayed there for about an hour and a half before returning to my wife, and during their break both Mark and Dave came and sat with me. We all passed on good comments about each other and I told them of my intentions regarding finishing The Sneakers, and both said what a shame but understood my reasoning and respected that. I told them that I would be making an announcement after I managed to cancel any bookings that would be affected, and could they keep it to themselves until it was public?

I sent e-mails to Brett, the owner of the Riviera Hotel Torquay, telling him that we were finishing at Christmas and that we would not be able to play at one of his other hotels at Babbacombe for the New Year's Eve celebrations. I did not receive a response and wondered whether it had been seen. I gave it a week and then sent another e-mail, this time to the hotel enclosing the message previously sent: again no reply. I then gave it a couple of days and then messaged the entertainments manager Chris Chaplin who had the decency to reply, telling me that Brett had received the original message: to say I was not impressed is an understatement! We were not under contract and I had given six months' notice.

As I have said, I had told a few friends of our intentions but I was to make an announcement at our next gig, as I knew we would be offered bookings for 2020 and that I would have to decline them. This booking was at St Annes Boardmills, one of our favourite gigs. I told Dave Plenty before our first session and he expressed genuine disappointment, and went on to tell me about a couple of other bands that were finishing this year. We went onstage and had a brilliant night. It went around the club that we were finishing, and at the end of the night lots of people came up to us and said it was sad as we were one of the best bands that they had ever heard. A table of four people called me over just after I had finished the first set playing 'Wipe Out' and said that we were the most 'POLISHED AND PROFESSIONAL BAND THAT EVER PLAYED ST ANNES AND THAT I WAS THE BEST DRUMMER THAT THEY HAD EVER SEEN' (I obviously told them that they were talking rubbish). They were very impressed with us, and also when I told them we were finishing were disappointed. The following day I put a post on Facebook using a draft that I had printed out:

THE SNEAKERS

The Sneakers have decided to finish at the end of this year. The band has been together many years: in fact, Paul and Billy have played in bands together since 1998. The band as they are now plus Dave Stock who only retired at the end of 2017 got together approx. 2002 and were called The Sultans. Previous to that Alan Braithwaite was lead guitarist. The band ran with two line-ups for a while but when Alan finished the name got changed to The Sneakers which was the name of the band Chris was in years before. We have decided to finish at the end of year as Chris has C.O.P.D. and is beginning to find breathing difficult. Billy wants to move back to Scotland and Paul at seventy-one doesn't want the stress of running a band and all the travelling and organising that goes with the successful running of a band. We aim to finish on a high and all bookings that we have had to cancel after Christmas have been notified.
We have a very loyal following and we would like to thank you all for your support over the years.
Many thanks, Paul, Billy and Chris
The Sneakers

and the response was incredible: I had friends, fellow musicians entertainment managers, you name it, all saying what a brilliant band The Sneakers are and how much they would be missed (I actually had a tear when reading some of the comments and was too choked to read them out loud). My wife took the printout to Timsbury British Legion on the Saturday night as we were playing St Annes and she said the response was incredible and that we would be terribly missed.

I was supposed to practise for three weeks with Roger and Annie

Paul Brimble

Davenport and Gary, their bass player. Well, that has turned into four and they have asked me to do the next week as well. To be quite honest, I am really enjoying it as it has taken me out of my comfort zone, and I didn't realise I could play these other styles of music with so much ease and was fitting in so well with the other players.

The Sneakers played a 70th birthday party at Midsomer Norton Social Club where there were a few of our followers. There would have been a lot more if I hadn't encouraged a lot not to come as it was a private party and, if not invited, it would not be fair on the guests if they couldn't get seats, and as it turned out I was right.

Monday night was jam night at The White Hart and I had agreed to set the drums up in the afternoon. Roger was already there when I arrived and was moving some tables to make room for the back line of amplifiers. Billy turned up just in time to help wire up the bass rig, and all was now set for the evening jam session. The White Hart has a private smoking area at the rear of the pub and it has a glass floor over the River Somer which runs virtually under the pub and right down through the middle of Midsomer Norton.

I stayed there for quite a while talking over old times with the owner of the pub, Sue, mostly about the Court Hotel which she used to own previously, and spoke about the band The Honky-Tonks that used to practise there and also about Andrew, her husband who used to be their lead guitarist.

I got to the jam session about 7.30pm. Roger, Annie and Paul Kirtley were already there so that I virtually just sat on the kit and played. Annie, who is a very talented sax player, picked up the bass guitar and just played it to my amazement!

The jam session was good, possibly because Paul Kirtley took charge, or even possibly despite it, as Paul can be a bit of a hogger! Roger had decided in the afternoon that three guitar amplifiers would be enough and that it would stop too many guitarists playing at the same time (hopefully this is what will be adopted for all future jams) and it worked. Taffy and Dylan turned up, as did Billy, Charlie and Mike Goodliffe also another sax player and a singer, all helped to make it one of the best sessions so far. I actually was approached by a band that night to join them, but I told them I was keeping my options open and I wasn't making any commitments anytime soon. I was going to finish with The Sneakers first and possibly take a break from playing until I could get my head around my future.

Wednesday was my last rehearsal with Roger Davenport and at the end I was thanked and also told that they wished I was in a position to join them, but that they respected what I was doing and also that I really helped them to get a tight show together.

Saturday I arranged to pick Billy up and we set off to Bishopsworth to put our gear up for our evening performance. Often we would set up lunchtimes: it took the pressure off the gig. Obviously C.J. couldn't as he had to drive up from Weymouth but he would then pick up Billy on the way through and I would drive the van straight to the gig. I was glad to pick up Billy as he was to tell me that his mixer had been repaired and that he had used it the night before with no problems.

The gig was a good one and when Bob March, the entertainments manager, introduced us he also told the almost full house that we were finishing at the end of the year and the reaction was immense: we had a lot of comments made to all three of us during our break and at the end of the night. We also had three encores and eventually finished with 'Penny Arcade', which turned out to be one of the club's favourite songs (mind you, we already knew that!). A lot of people wanted to talk to us at the end of the night and we had some lovely comments. I really was in a hurry to go home but, as I have already said many times, 'We Live On Accolades!'

Because of my heart problems in the past I have been chosen to be an official speaker for the British Heart Foundation and I did a talk this week at Farmborough Goodwill Club and was assured that my talk went down well. Two ladies came up afterwards and gave me donations as well as what the

Paul Brimble

organisation had given me, all was banked the following day into the British Heart Foundation account.

Our next booking was Timsbury British Legion on the following Saturday, and there was also an 80th birthday party as well as open club night. To say the club was packed would be an understatement: there must have been in excess of 200 people! We had an excellent night with a lot of people saying that The Sneakers will be well missed when we finish. Our last night will be at Timsbury Legion, and I think it will be packed to the rafters.

The following Thursday we were to play at Welton Rovers Football Club for the monthly social put on by Midsomer Norton: it was a very hot afternoon but even so quite a full house attended. Chris was not available for this gig, as he had to have a camera inserted regarding his health problems, and I managed to get Frank Aust to cover for him and he played a blinder! We still have a couple more Thursday afternoon socials to do before we finish.

Frank invited me to a gig he was playing on the following Saturday and, as I was free, went to watch him and his band play. I walked in The King William IV pub at Combe Down, Bath, and before I could order a drink was called up to where the band were playing by the drummer Pedro (a very talented and colourful character) and proceeded to play a couple of songs with Frank. My old mate Tony Poole was playing bass as a guest also and Mike Nash, a very good singer, was doing the vocals also guesting. For the second song I played Steve White, the old man from Old Man's Hat, played bass and he also sang the vocal. Later on that evening I got up with an old friend of mine, Brian Stritcher, doing the vocals on about four songs; he, like myself, has suffered a stroke, with his more disabilitating than mine, but he has been left with a good attitude. I enjoyed playing with all these other people, but when I watch people like Pedro play it brings me well down to earth.

On the third Monday of each month there is a jam session at The White Hart pub Midsomer Norton where quite a lot of musicians turn up to play. Over the years I have met and made a lot of musician friends. This

My Life with Music

session there was only two drummers and I got to play with most of the visiting musicians as Mike, the other drummer, didn't get there until late and preferred to drink rather than play, but that was fine by me. Roger, Annie, Billy and myself played three songs which all of us except Billy had previously rehearsed: we were so tight that we brought the house down. The whole session was good and I managed to play songs that I hadn't done for years some that I really had to think about but we got away with it by the seat of our pants!

I was invited to a party at the Waggon & Horses, Peasedown St John for one of our friends' brother: it was a party given to him as he was going back to Australia where he lives. As the date got closer I was asked if I would like to back the singer guitarist on drums for the night, and as it was my old mate Brian Talbot how could I refuse? Not that I wanted to. When I got to the pub to set up, the heavens opened and I was like a drowned rat! The gig turned out to be very good and Brian told me it was by far the best night that he had enjoyed for many years, which really made my night.

The following weekend The Sneakers played on the Sunday which was most unusual for us as we normally played on the Friday or Saturday, and this was for a golden wedding for a couple that I knew quite well. I had been warned that there was to be a very well-known guest invited, a certain Mr Michael Eavis, the person responsible for the Glastonbury Festival, and sure enough he was there. Talk about eccentric: he had a suit on above the waist and shorts and sandals beneath, but with his famous profile it was normal for him to dress like this!

We were back to one of our regular gigs the following Friday at Midsomer Norton Social Club where, according to our audience, we had a really good sound and the place was buzzing. We are one of only two live bands that play this club: they normally have solo acts but when we play we seem to get a much bigger audience than them. At the end of the night I loaded all of Billy's kit into the van and as I stacked it right up to the roof of the van didn't realise that I had left the lights on as I couldn't see them. I had a bit of a shock the following afternoon. I was having a rest when the van alarm went off. I went out expecting the windscreen camera had fallen off as it had in the past to cause the alarm to activate, but to my horror there was not enough battery left to get in the van. I got into a terrible state wondering how I could get in the van and, as I had all Billy's kit, how could we do tonight's gig!? I rang my breakdown service and they were to arrange a repair if possible but in the meantime my son-in-law turned up and said that he had some heavy-duty jump leads: all we had to do was somehow get them connected. In the meantime I decided that I would try to get in the van through the side sliding window. Image 89 This window is about fourteen inches square, but because I had lost over four stones I managed to get in and then I climbed into the front and managed to get the bonnet open only to find that the battery isn't under the bonnet, it's under the passenger's side floor!

The van window that I had to climb through

We managed to get the leads connected and started the van. In the meantime Maurice Day, the organiser for that evening's gig, had rung to say that because of the weather we would be playing in their clubhouse, not on the back of a lorry as arranged. (I didn't have the heart to tell him we might not even get there, let alone worry about the weather.) I took the van for a twenty-minute drive to build up the battery and also stood down the breakdown service.

The gig turned out quite well, and as the weather calmed down we could have played on the lorry, but a decision had to be made earlier because of the electrics. When we got there a lady was singing and playing keyboards: it turned out that she was quite a good drummer also and that she had played for the Ivy Benson Band, an all-lady band very well known in the 60s and 70s. As I like to hear what my kit sounds like, I let her play a couple of songs. The night was good until the end when we had to put up with some rowdy people who had been drinking all day. One even fell over our stage lights, so we finished ten minutes early. These things happen, luckily not too often.

I had been rehearsing with Roger Davenport and the jam session was coming up. Billy my bass player was unable to attend so Roger's wife Annie had been talking to another bass player, Johny, who said he would play, and he turned out to be a tidy bass player and very keen, so much so that we all got together a couple of days later and decided we would like it to go further and Roger took a booking for us for about six weeks later.

This week I played a jam session where I did most of the drumming, a rehearsal and two gigs, the first being an eighteenth birthday party, and the following night we played Wyke Regis Working Men's Club at Weymouth.

The birthday party was for Knobby Collins, the man who was responsible for getting us loads of gigs at Waterside Holiday Park Bowleaze Cove Weymouth. He told the entertainment manager, 'You've got to get them Sneakers down here,' and the rest is history! We got to play at least eight venues in Weymouth over the following years, but at the time of me writing this we were down to only one, and that is the Wyke Regis Working Men's Club where we are always well received. That will be the penultimate gig, the last Saturday before Christmas for The Sneakers, as we play our last gig in front of our local fans at Timsbury British Legion on New Year's Eve.

Talking about Timsbury British Legion, we played here after Wyke and this is a club that has solo acts most weeks. In fact to my knowledge

Paul Brimble

The Sneakers are the only band that play this club and some Saturdays the audience numbers are dire, but for some reason when we play there it is always packed. I cannot remember one night that the venue was not packed for us, so much so that other venues in the area avoided booking expensive acts when we were playing locally. We had a brilliant night and a lot of people were already seated before I got there but at this club I always set up most of our kit during lunchtime. At the end of the evening we gave a long encore which was warmly received and appreciated, and it took ages to take our kit down and load up due to people talking to us, and what a good night they had had and what were we going to do when we retire?

The following week was to be our farewell weekend at Torquay: we had played numerous weekends and New Year's dates since 2003 in three different hotels, albeit one of the hotels changed its name because of change of ownership.

The first hotel was the Bute Court and was a medium-sized hotel with 47 rooms; the second was the Bishops Court Hotel, a much bigger hotel but further out of town. We then went back to the Bute Court and at the end of 2011 the Bute Court went bankrupt and nothing was booked in Torquay for 2012, which happened to be the year that I was incapacitated with my stroke. But towards the latter part of the year lots of our following were asking could we not find another hotel in Torquay. So I said I would see if I could organise one.

I managed to get the management of the Rainbow International Hotel interested in booking us, and our weekend with them was such a hit we were given two weekends each year for the following few years and also a couple of New Year bookings right up to when the hotel changed hands, and at the time of writing the hotel, now with its name changed to the Riviera Hotel, took us as we were changing virtually nothing as far as we were concerned and also giving us New Year's bookings as well.

This weekend was our last weekend before we retired, and I suppose it was sad for a lot of our followers as it had become like a little holiday for some of them. I write the programme for the Friday and Saturday nights, but the Sunday I leave up to the other two. Most years it turns out to be somewhat of a shambles for continuity and I am a bit of a stickler on that, so this weekend was no different: Friday brilliant night, Saturday brilliant night. Sunday the list was only written out for one and only in biro so nobody was sure what to play next. But when we had our break I took over and sorted out the songs that we hadn't yet played and highlighted out the ones that we have already done as we don't repeat any songs. When you play three sets each night for three nights each set having approx fifteen songs: not a bad feat. Bernie Barret played with us, and even our wives got up to sing 'Mustang Sally'.

With our wives on stage at the Riviera Hotel Torquay

I turned the night around, and at the end of the night one of our followers got up on the microphone and paid a tearful tribute to The Sneakers for the many years that we had entertained so many people. Billy has bought an electric set of bagpipes and played 'Amazing Grace' before we finished the night with a Status Quo song and then with the many compliments from our old and our new friends it took ages to pack down our kit: in fact, I ended up having to do some of it in the morning!

The following Thursday The Sneakers played for the Midsomer Norton Community Trust at their first Thursday of the month social afternoon get-together. Ever since we were approached about playing the occasional afternoon for them the interest has built up and maintained quite well, and this one was good for the number of people. Also we had a very good, balanced sound by all accounts, which was good for me as a lot of the audience had been to Torquay with us the previous week. I have been asked if I can do three bookings for the following year for them and intend to use Billy and Frank with myself if they agree. They did and we are playing under the name of Spirelaine, which was the name of one of my previous bands.

The next booking was Haydon Que Club and it was to be our last gig there before we retired, and the club was packed; a lot of the audience were sad that The Sneakers were finishing and we had to tell them of our local bookings for the end of the year. We played well and it was a very good night. On the following Wednesday I did one of my British Heart Foundation talks and it was to a young wives' group. They might have been young when they were formed but the average age now was about 70, but by all accounts I did very well and my talk was very informative. I did know quite a few of the women there but that didn't make it any easier.

On Friday of that week we had a gig at Hythe near Southampton so had to pick up Billy at four in the afternoon for the long drive to get there. We had one of our best nights ever and the club was packed, people were saying it was a pity that it was our last time at the club, and at the end of the night we had a lot of photos taken with various people that we had made friends with over the years.

The following night I went to the Frome Memorial Theatre to see Joe Brown and thoroughly enjoyed his show. Joe played an electric acoustic guitar, banjo, ukulele and violin, and he even had a go on a piano accordion. I must admit that I would have liked him to play a solid electric guitar but the show was good and his fellow musicians were excellent: the drummer even played cardboard boxes with microphones in them the whole of the first half, and I was very impressed with the sound that he got!

Our next gig was the following Friday at Midsomer Norton Social Club. Billy and myself set the kit up at 9.00 in the morning which takes the pressure off us for the evening as it was the first Friday of the month which meant that bingo was to be played before we were to start. Chris was there before 7.00pm to set his gear up and we started at 9.00pm.

The night was good for us and we were well appreciated; according to some we were a bit loud but when we asked our regular followers we were told it was fine. We did a few songs that we don't normally do and they went down well.

Our farewell gigs continued the following week at Yeovil Labour Club, bearing in mind that we had to cancel the previous one because of things totally out of our control (Chris's father-in-law died the morning of the gig) and I was not able to get a dep player or another band to take our place, probably down to the fact it was a Bank Holiday weekend.

When we arrived at the Labour Club there was hardly anyone there and the ones that were there said that the club was now crap and the bands that they were booking were not aimed at their regular customers and most of the regulars had joined other clubs, only coming back to see bands like The Sneakers. As the night went on, the hall eventually was packed and at the end of the night we had loads of photos taken with various people.

Bernie Barrat, a long-time friend of the band, played rhythm guitar for us all night: he had previously played with us on our last night at the Riviera Hotel Torquay a few weeks before and he did quite well. The night went extremely well and, as usual, we had to do a couple of encores.

Some of our personal friends had been very ill and had through time overcome their illnesses. Dave Sparey had stomach cancer and the positive way he dealt with it was awesome. Mike Collins had his hip removed and ended up with some sort of metal filing blood poisoning and was in hospital for many months, and Keith Dallimore the man whose life I truly believe I saved when I brought him home from Torquay (this is already documented previously in the book). All three decided to have a survivors' party with The Sneakers to provide the entertainment, and Mary my wife was asked to make a cake and what a cake she came up with with the help of my daughter.

Mike Collins, Dave Sparey and Keith Dallimore

The following Monday was the jam session at The White Hart and was a very good night with the usual jammers: Roger, Billy, Kevin, Brian, Andrew, Annie, John, Doug and Mike. There was also a band, Avalon Highway (very good), and also a blind drummer Adam who managed to damage the snare drum head which I had warned Andrew, the landlord, was needing to be replaced anyway.

My Life with Music

Brian Talbot and me at The White Hart Jam Session

Me and Brian Talbot 40 years on

The Sneakers were by now well on their farewell tour of the clubs and hotels before they were to finish for good, and the next booking was at Whitchurch British Legion, not usually a gig to write home about but I made it well known on Facebook and locally that the room was a good size for dancing, and the audience, although not immense, were very appreciative towards us. I was very surprised on the night when in front of us was the largest that we had ever had in that club over the years that we had played there. Mind you, a lot of it was down to me as there were at least 25 people from our home town, but the icing on the cake was that Dave Clarke from The Two of Clubs, probably the most popular duo in the Bristol area at the time and a really nice person as well, was in the audience and he paid us some lovely comments at the end of the evening. He also sent me two videos that he had taken on his phone that night. Dave had never seen the band before but obviously seen videos of The Sneakers, and told us that the balance that we had was perfect! Dave said that he and Mark, the other half of the duo, would like to see us again before we finish, but with their workload I doubt that would happen.

The night went well and we were very happy with our sound: we seemed to be having an extremely good run and everybody wanted photos taken with us which is great but hinders us with the packing up of our kit at the end of the evening (not a problem for us, but often is with the bar staff!).

We shouldn't have favourite bookings but our next gig was at St Annes Boardmills, a club that all of the band would agree is one of the best clubs to play at. Dave Plenty, the man in charge of entertainment at the club, has put it back to the days where if you weren't there by seven in the evening you would be lucky if you could find a seat. The club has entertainment every Friday, Saturday and Sunday; we only play Saturdays as Fridays are normally cabaret night and Sundays solo acts, but by all accounts all nights are very popular.

Our night was advertised as our last at the club and it was absolutely packed. We had a very good night and were told that we were one of the most popular and professional bands that play there and would be sadly missed.

The following Thursday a band called Niteshift played the afternoon social at Welton Rovers. Mary and myself went along to see them as we prefer live bands to solo artists. I was very impressed with them as they had improved a lot since the last time that I had seen them. I knew two of the band: Barry the lead singer, and Keith the drummer. I am known for my drumming on 'Wipe Out', an instrumental number, but I thought Keith did a better job of it than me, but all my mates and my wife said that they could dance better to my version.

On the Saturday we played our first Christmas party and this was for Tony Day whom we did this booking for every year and had done for probably fifteen years or more! As usual, Billy and myself set the kit up in the morning and had to make room for ourselves, working around the Christmas trees and decorations. The entertainment the night before at the club was a singer that I had got to know well over the years and was very popular, but this particular week he had shot himself in the foot, as the saying goes. About three times a year he puts on a function in Trowbridge and gets a very good following from our local area which is about fifteen miles away, but this weekend he played Midsomer Norton Social Club on the Friday, entrance fee £1, and Saturday at Trowbridge £10, and The Sneakers were at Midsomer Norton Social Club: no entrance fee also a free buffet and our final appearance at that club.

I apologised to Russ, as I knew that most of his usual followers were coming to see us and he understood why. Another club suffered terribly that night and that was Timsbury British Legion: they only had six people in the club!

Tony's party went well and was packed out: even another band came to see us, a band called Hair of the Dog. Billy had taught their bass player, and Dave Riddle their drummer whom Chris knew from years ago, got up and he played 'All Right Now' on my kit and I thought he did a very good job of it and it was good to hear my kit played well by someone else. We had many good compliments made to us on the night and lots of people said that we will be missed when we finish.

The Sneakers were classed as one of the most popular bands in the local area even, taking in Bristol; also well received in Torquay, Dawlish and, going the other direction, Southampton. The band had played a pretty broad range of bookings, taking in weddings, birthdays, private parties, Masonic, Rotary, Lions, the Buffalos. The band appeared at pubs, clubs, hotels, festivals, Mardi Gras, golf clubs, private gardens, and even a nudist colony in Hampshire.

We were now getting close to the end of the year and we were booked to play the Midsomer Norton Community Trust over-sixties Christmas party. I set up my drums on the Thursday night and Chris and Billy put their kit in Friday lunchtime ready for a 2.00pm start. The party went with a swing and was full to capacity, and the council pushed the boat out for the guests with a lovely buffet and loads of goodies and a selection box for all.

Mary went away to Torquay on the day of the party and was away until the Sunday, as it was her birthday weekend, and as I was playing bookings on both the Friday and the Saturday she decided to go away with friends of ours to see a couple of tribute acts. They were disappointed with the Elvis on the Friday, but the Saturday one was very good by all accounts!

Saturday morning I had a phone call: Chris was too ill to play that night and could I get Frank to help out as he didn't think he would be well enough to play at Dawlish that night? It proved to me that The Sneakers retiring was the right decision, and if I had any doubts not to worry as I had made the right decision. Frank was not available and he suggested that I contacted Dave Stock who had left the band two years earlier and had said at the time that he was giving up playing the guitar for good as he had problems with his fingers etc. But being a trouper he saved the night!

It caused me no end of problems, though, as I had to pick up his kit and write a list of songs that we would be confident to play. Luckily we had to share the night with a disco and just as well, as there were 185 people booked in for the Christmas party that we were playing. Dave did us well and we got by: it was different but it worked and we even had to do an encore!

As usual we were fed with their finest three-course meal and were treated the same as their paying guests, and we got paid with no quibble at the end of the evening and I was thanked personally for not letting them down and supplying entertainment when I could have cancelled at the last minute but sorted it myself.

I wasn't sorry when I got home after that gig as it's the best part of a fourteen-hour shift by the time that I had picked up Dave and then Billy plus all of his kit, and then to drive 92 miles each way, set up, take down and repeat the journey home. Why do we do it?! Never mind, I was in bed at 3.30am.

I felt bad for Mary and took her away to Bournemouth for two nights as a birthday treat the following week.

We were booked to play Wyke Regis the following Saturday. It was a gig we always looked forward to but this time it was a bit flat. We were concerned that it was us, but we were told that the club had a Christmas party the night before, and a lot of our usual following were there and wouldn't go out two nights on the trot.

Christmas 2019 had now arrived and this was to be my last year in a committed band. I am sure that I will regret packing in The Sneakers as we were a busy, hard-working popular act and at the top of our game, but I was to be proved right in my decision to finish the band as the reasons for finishing were: (a) I had had enough of being the organiser of the band and this situation hasn't changed; (b) Chris's health and that situation was getting worse; and (c) Billy wants to move back to Scotland, and the only thing stopping him was his elderly mother-in-law, but sadly she died on the 5th January and he really has nothing to stop him from going.

I am going to finish this book now, even though I was intending it to be about 50 years of me and my music, but because of what happened to me at the end of 2011 with my stroke and my journey with music afterwards, I have extended it up to New Year's Eve 2019, the last time that I officially played with The Sneakers.

I had arranged to play our final gig at Timsbury British Legion so that we could be in front of our loyal local following. I was surprised when I announced we were to finish that Dave, who had retired from the band, asked me if he could play our last night with us, but not to tell anyone! That proved to be a hard task as lots of our following were suggesting Dave should play but I had to play it down for Dave's sake.

We were able to set up in the morning two on the stage (Chris and Paul) and two on the floor (Dave and Billy): we had to be careful not to block the fire exit!

As Chris had to drive up from Weymouth, he was to set up at night. I drove the van that night and took some of our friends so that they could have a drink. Dave brought some backing tracks so that he could start the night off with some Shadows songs for about 40 minutes before the full band took over. We were well received and played a blinder: all of us were on form and the night went well. I have spoken to a lot of the audience since, and all but none said how much they had enjoyed the night and most added their regrets that we were not to play again.

We had a bit of fun playing a couple of comedy songs up to the countdown at midnight, getting everyone in a circle ready for 'Auld Lang Syne' and Billy playing his bagpipes. We then had a five-minute break and brought the house down rocking the place until 1.15am after a couple of encores, and spent about an hour talking to all.

Chris and Billy took their kit that night but Dave and myself left our kit on the stage for me to pick up later that week. During the evening Elaine, Dave's wife, did a speech which was really aimed at me as a thankyou for all the gigs and for taking Dave and her, also Mary, my wife, in the van to the gigs. She was shaking like a leaf and kept getting lost and repeating herself but bless her, she did her best. I took over the mike and gave a bit of a rendition of the origins of the band and I was well received. I also got a lovely speech done for me and The Sneakers by Elaine on behalf of Timsbury British Legion.

I would like to say how much I have enjoyed my life with music, and would like to thank my understanding wife Mary and all the musicians that I have had the good luck of working with from when I was at school to my early bands, right through to now and hopefully beyond. It has certainly been *My Life With Music*.